SHIPWRECK

& 60,00

SHIPWRECK, SAILORS & 60,000 YEARS

1778 and all that happened before then

Jackie French

Illustrations and cartoons by

Peter Sheehan

A Scholastic Press book
from Scholastic Australia

Scholastic Press
345 Pacific Highway
Lindfield NSW 2070
an imprint of Scholastic Australia Pty Limited (ABN 11 000 614 577)
PO Box 579
Gosford NSW 2250
www.scholastic.com.au

Part of the Scholastic Group
Sydney • Auckland • New York • Toronto • London • Mexico City
• New Delhi • Hong Kong • Buenos Aires • Puerto Rico

First published by Scholastic Press in 2006.
This edition published in 2009.

Illustrations and cartoons by Peter Sheehan.
Internal design and typesetting by Lake Shore Graphics.

Historical Advisor/Editor, Dr Bruce Scates, A/Professor of History,
University of New South Wales.

National Library of Australia Cataloguing-in-Publication entry

French, Jackie.
Shipwreck, sailors & 60,000 years.
For upper primary/lower secondary students.
ISBN 978-1-74169-313-3.
1. Australia - History - To 1788 - Juvenile literature.
I. Sheehan, Peter, 1964- . II. Title. (Series : French,
Jackie. Fair dinkum histories).

994.01

Typeset in 11.5/15pt Espirit Book.

Printed by McPherson's Printing Group, Victoria.

10 9 8 7 6 5 4 12 13 14 15 / 1

Contents

Digging the Dirt on the Dim Distant Past

How can we know what happened sixty thousand years ago?

Sometimes we can get an idea from stories passed down for generations. Sometimes scientists use techniques to work out things such as the age of tools, bones or rock engravings; or how long it's been since Aboriginal people spoke the same language; or how many generations of dingoes have lived in Australia.

But these facts only give us part of the picture. We still don't know much of the past for certain. We can't even say for sure whether humans came here 45 000 or 60 000 years ago. We will never know the names of those who first stepped onto Australian soil.

Who invented the boomerang?

Was it the Portuguese or the Chinese who saw Australia before the Dutch?

This book is as accurate as our team can make it. But tomorrow new evidence might be dug up. Or, maybe, in twenty years time, you might find an ancient map. If that happens, the way we look at our past may completely change.

But until those discoveries are made, we've done our best in *Shipwreck, Sailors & 60,000 Years* to give you a glimpse into the extraordinary world of yesterday.

CHAPTER 1

ARE WE THERE YET?

This is the story of perhaps sixty thousand years of Australian history. It tells how the land was discovered by the early Aboriginal people; how they explored and settled; and how they became separate nations with their own languages and ways of life.

For nearly all of those sixty thousand years, most of the people on our planet knew about only their own small part of the world. For a very long time hardly anyone visited the great continent in the south. Most people didn't even know it was there. Eventually traders and explorers from China, Spain, Portugal, Holland, France, Indonesia and Britain would 'discover' Australia over and over again. Some of them would even claim it as their own.

Some Aboriginal histories describe how Aboriginal people have always lived here, from the time the land was formed.

THE FIRST HUMAN FOOTPRINT

The first journey to Australia was probably the longest journey in the world. Scientists think that the first humans came from Africa more than 100 000 years ago. Gradually, over tens of thousands of years, some of them crossed into Europe then headed across the Middle East, central Asia and India before travelling down the coasts of South-East Asia. Some of *their* descendants became the world's first great ocean voyagers.

Over even more thousands of years, with no maps to guide them, some of *their* descendants sailed from island to island, reef to reef, until they came to the islands north of Australia, perhaps to what are now Indonesia and Timor.

Why did they keep going?

Maybe they saw far-off smoke from bushfires drifting above the horizon. Maybe they saw land birds flying in from the ocean and realised that there must be land to the south. Maybe a tsunami or volcano destroyed their land, and they were forced to look for somewhere else to live. Perhaps these people were fishing and found the continent by accident—a raft blown by monsoon winds from Timor will arrive on the Australian coast about ten days later. Perhaps they were traders or adventurers, longing to know what lay beyond the horizon.

What we do know is that those ancient people came from across the sea. Sixty thousand years ago the sea level was far lower than it is now. But there would still have been at least sixty-five kilometres of islands and mangrove swamps between the lands now known as New Guinea and Cape York, and there was never a time when someone could walk or swim across this strait.

WEIRD AND WONDERFUL

The new land had some strange creatures—hippo-sized wombat-like diprotodons, marsupial lions, and pythons five metres long. It was a dangerous land, with giant crocodiles and poisonous fish, huge carnivorous goannas and venomous snakes.

The lush northern landscape these people arrived in was much like the lands they had left behind. But over thousands of years their descendants slowly explored the rest of this giant continent, where they faced new dangers, and learnt to cope in harsh deserts and snow-covered mountains.

The oldest camp sites that have been found so far are at Malakunanja and Nauwalabila in Arnhem Land in the Northern Territory. They could be over fifty thousand years old.

History Mysteries

Scientists study genetics to work out people's ancestries and where they came from. These studies suggest that some of the first Australians were descended from people who lived in what is now Taiwan, and that they came here through the Philippines and modern Indonesia. These people could have arrived in Australia between forty and seventy thousand years ago. But ancient Australia may also have been settled by more than one group of people.

Some stories are told from person to person. This is called oral history. Aboriginal oral histories tell of ancient volcanic explosions, giant animals and long-ago tsunamis.

The Gagadju people of the Alligator River area in the Northern Territory tell of their great ancestress, Imberombera, who came from across the sea. Her womb was full of children, and she carried woven bags on her head filled with yams, seeds and plants. The Gunwinggu people tell of their ancestress, Waramurungundji, who also came from across the sea—from the north-west, where modern Timor and Indonesia are. Like Imberombera, she came in a canoe.

Telling the Stories

Aboriginal people have their own stories about the history of their land. Some of the stories are secret and sacred knowledge, and can't be shared with outsiders, as they belong to the people who inherited them.

Other stories have been shared with the world. Some of these stories tell us how Aboriginal people's ancestors came from the sea; other stories say that Aboriginal people come from beings that have always been part of the country.

The early history of Australia is sometimes referred to as happening *in the Dreamtime*. Dreaming and Dreamtime are difficult ideas to understand. Dreaming can mean history, or it can mean a story about long-ago events. Sometimes it refers to the ancient stories of creation by Dreamtime beings. It can also refer to the law that was handed down long ago.

Many Aboriginal people don't like to use these terms, as they imply that their history and beliefs are vague or half-forgotten—like dreams.

GETTING A DATE

There are two main scientific ways of working out how old things are: *radiocarbon dating* and *thermoluminescence dating*.

All living things absorb a little radioactive carbon from the atmosphere. When the plant or animal dies it stops absorbing it, and the radioactive carbon starts to decay. The amount of radioactive carbon present in an ancient bone today will tell us how old that bone is.

Thermoluminescence dating is also based on radioactivity. Most minerals store energy from sunlight or artificial radioactivity. This stored energy can be released as a glow, or thermoluminescence. A piece of pottery, for example, will gradually absorb energy from the moment it is fired, and scientists can work out how old it is by measuring the amount of thermoluminescence it gives off when they heat it up again.

But the dates we get from these methods aren't exact. They simply give a range of possible dates, such as 'between forty and fifty thousand years ago', which give us a broad idea of when things might have happened.

What! No Elephants?

A stretch of water once divided the ancient continent of Sahul (Australia and New Guinea) from Sunda (the super-continent of Indonesia and South-East Asia). This stretch of water is like a dividing line that prevented Australian marsupials from wandering north into Asia—and stopped elephants and orang-outangs from marching south into Australia. Scientists refer to this as the Wallace Line.

Ancient Axes

The people who settled Australia and New Guinea may have been the most advanced toolmakers in the world. Archaeologists have found what may be the world's earliest *hafted* stone axe on the north coast of Papua New Guinea. A hafted axe-head is one that has been shaped to be fixed to a handle.

Strangers in a Strange Land

We know that the early people of Australia were incredible explorers. We know they could survive everything from snowy mountains to harsh deserts—and could adapt to the changes of the ice age too. We know they were skilled artists. Australian art is amongst the earliest in the world. We know that they probably had some form of religion: by thirty thousand years ago they buried their dead with ritual. We know they had stone tools as advanced as anywhere in the world.

We even know they were great traders. Darwin glass, a hard rock that came from a meteor crater in the Northern Territory, was traded in places as far away as Tasmania.

But we will never know these people's names, or what they felt about the extraordinary things they saw and did. There are no records that go back that far, and the culture of later Aboriginal people doesn't reveal much about how their long-ago ancestors might have lived.

WERE THERE NEANDERTHAL PEOPLE IN AUSTRALIA?

Probably not. The ancestors of Aboriginal Australians were *Homo sapiens*, just as *Homo sapiens* are the ancestors of all humans today. The Neanderthal people were a group of *Homo erectus*, who were ancient cousins of *Homo sapiens*, and were named after the Neanderthal Valley in Europe where their fossils were first found.

Fossils of tiny people have been found on the islands of Java and Flores just north of Australia. Many scientists think that these tiny 'hobbits' were living on Flores as recently as twelve thousand years ago. (These metre-tall 'hobbits' hunted miniature mammoths, and were probably wiped out by a volcano.) The 'hobbits' were thought to be *Homo erectus*, but scientists now think they may be descended from the far more ancient *australopithecus*.

The Flores people would have needed boats to reach their island, so maybe they would have been able to reach Australia too. But no evidence has been found yet to prove that they did.

A Long Way Home

The journey to Australia was probably the longest that humans had ever made. It crossed great continents and took tens of thousands of years. This journey also included perhaps the longest sea crossings ever made so far—crossings from one island to the next in rafts and flimsy canoes. Those who landed on the northern Australian coastline probably never realised that they had reached a huge continent instead of just another island.

CHAPTER 2

MOVING IN

We don't know how soon those ancient people started to explore the continent. Maybe they stayed in the north for many generations, where the plants and animals were more like those their ancestors knew. But we do know that people eventually spread out across the entire continent of Australia.

By thirty thousand years ago there were people in Arnhem Land, Cape York, the far south of Western Australia, southern New South Wales, Victoria and the south of Tasmania. By twenty thousand years ago Aboriginal people had settled over the whole of Australia.

Perhaps people first followed the coasts, and then walked inland along the rivers. But they may also have headed directly into Central Australia. Central Australia was much wetter in those days. The dry lakes of today were full of water then, and were rich in fish, shellfish, ducks and other wildlife.

Picture of an Ancient World

Lake Mungo is now a dry, salt-lake bed. It is perfect for preserving ancient skeletons and tools, making it an extraordinary window through which we can see how ancient people lived.

Forty thousand years ago Lake Mungo and the Willandra Lakes were brimming with fresh water, full of fish and waterbirds, and edged by enormous sand dunes that sheltered the people from the wind. By looking at these people's skeletons, tools, and the bones from their rubbish heaps, we can work out how they lived.

It was a good and rich life by Lake Mungo. People lived mostly by the shores of the lake, but they also had temporary camps in places where they went to hunt for other foods, gather different roots, collect emu eggs or harvest grass seeds to make flour. They made an enormous range of stone tools; they made fishing nets; they gathered ochre; traded with faraway tribes; cooked in ground-ovens; and cremated and buried their dead with complex funeral rites.

More Settlers

Central Australia was occupied at least 22 000 years ago. At some stage during those many thousands of years more settlers probably arrived on the continent—but we don't know exactly when they came, or where they came from. Maybe there was only one group of people, or maybe there were several groups. They may have been physically different from the first inhabitants, but no-one is sure.

Footprints in the Sands of Time

Sometime between 23 000 and 19 000 years ago a small group of people walked across some squishy clay at Willandra Lakes in western New South Wales, and left behind their footprints. The group included kids who ran about while the grown-ups walked in single file. Their footprints hardened in the clay and were eventually covered with sand. The Willandra footprints are the largest collection of prints that old anywhere in the world.

Baby, It's Cold Outside

But then came the ice age—and the world started getting colder.

During the ice age vast areas of Europe and Asia were covered with ice for most of the year. Switzerland, Scandinavia, Canada and most of North America were mostly ice. So much ocean water was locked up in ice that the sea level was much lower than it is now, and many continents were connected by land bridges.

Aboriginal oral histories tell of volcanic eruptions that happened more than ten thousand years ago on the Atherton Tablelands in Queensland and in Victoria. They also tell of the separation of Kangaroo Island from mainland South Australia, which happened because of rising sea levels after the ice age.

Between 25 000 and 15 000 years ago, glaciers covered parts of Tasmania, as well as the Snowy Mountains in Victoria and New South Wales. As more water was locked up in the ice caps, the continent became drier. The people learnt how to adapt to both the cold and the dry, and these conditions affected them in more ways than one. Groups of people were separated by deserts and glaciers, as well as by distance. Stories and tools and customs became different, and distinct cultures began to appear. Their languages slowly evolved until people from one part of the country wouldn't have been able to understand those from other parts.

About fifteen thousand years ago the world warmed up again, and the ice began to melt. The water flowed back into the oceans, and the seas started rising. The lands along the coast began to vanish under the water.

Case of the Missing Megafauna

The first Australians arrived too late to meet the *Dromornis stirtoni*. It was a flightless bird, three metres or more in height, which probably weighed more than a half a tonne. *Dromornis stirtoni* may hold the record for being the biggest bird ever to walk the earth.

But the first Australians encountered other giant birds and animals. There was the massive short-faced kangaroo (*Diprotodon optatum*); the giant python (*Wonambi naracoortensis*), nearly a metre in diameter and about five metres long; and an emu-like flightless creature (*Genyornis newtoni*) that stood two metres tall and was twice as heavy as a modern-day emu.

But by about ten thousand years ago every creature taller than a human had vanished. What happened to them? Did they die out when the land grew colder and drier during the ice age? Or when people began to manage the land with fire? Could humans have hunted so many of them that they all died out? (In fact, none of the ancient camp sites contain megafauna bones, though there are fish bones and the bones of other animals.)

Maybe the extinction of the megafauna was due to a combination of several reasons. We will need to uncover many more clues before we really know.

Stories are still told of ancient giant beasts, like the monster Kadimakara in Central Australia that roamed the landscape during the Pleistocene period.

CHAPTER 3

AFTER THE ICE AGE

The end of the ice age came slowly, starting about fifteen thousand years ago. By about twelve thousand years ago glaciers were melting all around the world. The seas began to rise—a lot.

For many years people mightn't have noticed much of a change, as the sea rose only a centimetre or two a year. But then the sea would rise just enough to wash over the top of a sand dune, and water would suddenly rush in to swallow up all the nearby low-lying land. A single storm could flood inland for several kilometres—and then the flood waters would never go away. It must have been a terrifying time. Even in one lifetime, the changes would have been enormous.

In northern Australia at this time five kilometres of coastland vanished every year. In the south, land along the Great Australian Bight disappeared at the rate of about one kilometre a year. Eventually about one-seventh of what had been Australia vanished beneath the sea. That's about two-and-a-half million square kilometres, or an area the size of Western Australia.

There are many Aboriginal histories of this time: tales of how peninsulas became islands, how low-lying islands and reefs disappeared completely, and of how people starved. Elsewhere in the world, England and Ireland were separated from Europe by the rising sea. Sri Lanka was separated from India; Taiwan and the Philippines were cut off from China; and eastern Russia was cut off from North America.

Tasmania was cut off from the mainland about eight thousand years ago, creating Bass Strait and the islands there. New Guinea was also completely separated from Australia about eight thousand years ago. Mountains along the Queensland coast turned into the islands we know today.

A Changing World

As the ice melted, the paradise of lakes and grasslands in Central Australia began to dry up. The birds, fish and shellfish vanished. People ate more wild grains and big animals instead. But the land grew drier still. People had to move to wetter areas, or else work out new ways to survive.

At the same time, the seas kept rising steadily until about seven thousand years ago. Then they rose slowly for about another two thousand years. About five thousand years ago the seas finally stopped rising.

The Great Tool Revolution

For the thousands of years while the sea levels were rising, the tools that people used didn't change. Then, about four to five thousand years ago, there was a period of many inventions and much cultural change. Maybe a fresh wave of immigrants had arrived from newly flooded lands to the north, bringing new tools and ideas. Or maybe, now that the sea was no longer rising, people didn't have to worry about finding ways of living in new landscapes, and had more time to think of other things

The earliest stone tools were mostly rocks that had been chipped or ground into shape. People held these rocks directly in their hands, and these early tools were much the same all over Australia. After the ice age, tools became smaller. There were special tools for different jobs, and people now gave tools handles. Each region had its own tools. People travelled vast distances to trade for ready-made tools, or to trade for special stone, shells or wood to make their own.

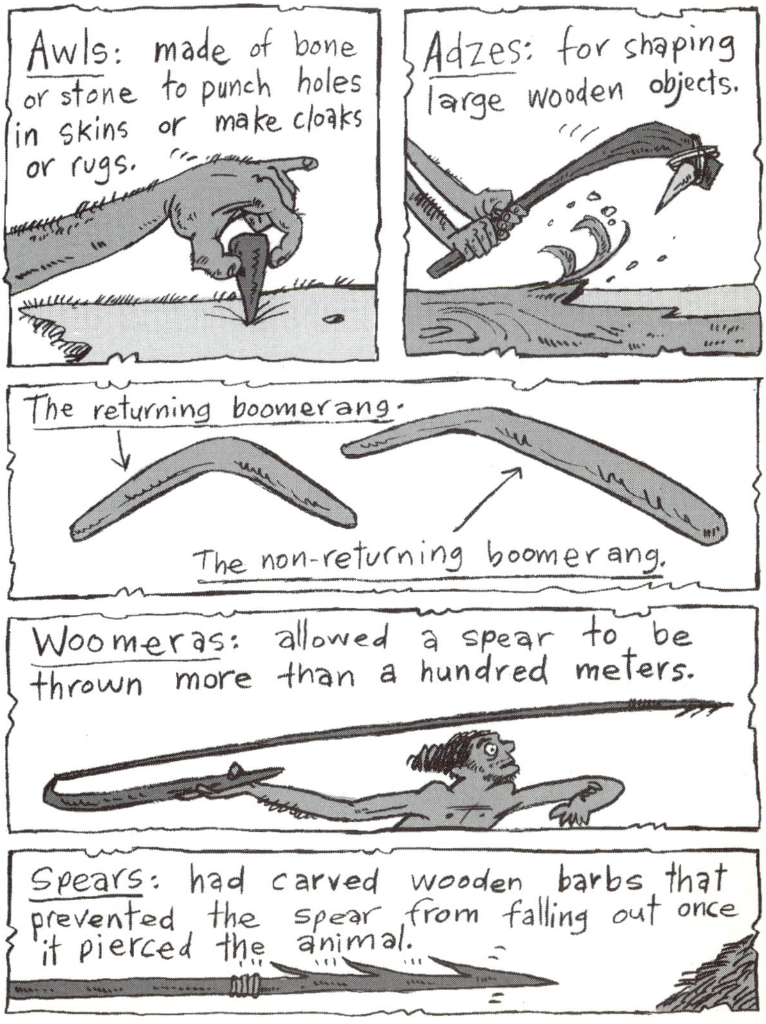

Emus can't be trained to pull a plough. You can't ride on a kangaroo. You can't breed platypus to lay more eggs, possums are hopeless as guard animals, and wombats won't carry your bag—even if you ask them nicely. In other parts of the world, people were keeping chickens, shearing sheep and riding horses. But until the dingo arrived, no animal in Australia could be domesticated.

One Big Farm

Farming started in Papua New Guinea about nine thousand years ago, when it was still partly joined to Australia. But farming never spread south from there.

Instead, Aboriginal people worked out ways of caring for the land so it would provide plenty of food without having to be farmed for it. They worked out how to predict the weather years in advance, so they'd know what food to gather and what to leave. They invented better ways of hunting, and found ways to get rid of poisons in roots and fruits.

Food could be found in every part of Australia. Even deserts and mountains were visited at certain times of the year for hunting and food gathering.

Now that there were better tools and more food, the land could support more people. Groups of people could settle in the same place for longer periods without having to move on to find fresh food supplies. In some places, small villages developed where people could live for most of the year.

The Dingo's Tale

Dingoes came to Australia four to five thousand years ago. They may have arrived with seafaring people who visited the north of Australia to trade for fine tools. They may also have arrived with a new wave of immigrants who came to settle in Australia.

The earliest dingo fossil is of a puppy, and is about 3500 years old.

All dingoes are descended from just a very small number of animals—possibly a single pregnant female that came ashore with traders or new settlers to have her pups. Dingoes are perhaps the oldest dog breed in the world, and they are the link between modern dogs and wolves. The ancestors of dingoes are the Asian wild dogs that still exist in South-East Asia today.

Modern dogs evolved from dingo ancestors, though this didn't happen in Australia. Dingoes were never bred to create different breeds. But there are different strains of dingo with a range of colours; for example, the south-eastern Highland Dingo, and the Old south-eastern Highland Dingo.

Over the next five thousand years dingoes became wild and spread to all parts of the Australian mainland, though they never made it to Tasmania—by the time the dingoes arrived, the land bridge between the mainland and Tasmania was gone. Some people believe that dingoes killed all the mainland Thylacines (Tasmanian tigers) and Tasmanian devils. But both survived in Tasmania—at least until white men arrived.

Dingoes were used for hunting. Dogs can track far more efficiently than humans, and they can run faster too. Dingoes were also companions and playmates. Women who had lost a child might carry one for comfort. In areas like the Snowy Mountains and Central Australia, where the night temperatures are very cold, dingoes were valued for their warmth. A particularly cold night in Central Australia is still sometimes called 'a five-dingo night'.

Digging up the Past

If everyone on Earth disappeared tomorrow, a visiting alien could learn a lot about modern culture simply by working out how to read our books.

But most Aboriginal culture was passed down in songs and stories and dances. Nothing was written down, and therefore much Aboriginal history has vanished. So what is left for us to study?

There is a lot for us to study. Just as an alien could learn about modern human culture by looking at our cities, we can study the culture of early Australians by looking at what they have left behind. Sometimes we can also guess how these ancient people lived, based on the way the Aboriginal people lived more recently.

True Blue Clues

Ceremonial sites: Bora grounds were where many ceremonies took place. They were usually made up of two large circles—a bit like small football ovals—surrounded by an earth bank, which would be topped by a brushwood fence.

Wells: In dry country, both natural and man-made wells were covered with a slab of rock to stop the water evaporating. These wells show us where people used to live.

Fish traps: Fish traps on coastal beaches were mostly made of stone walls, often topped with timber or reed fences. The fish would swim behind the fences when the tide was high, and be trapped when the tide went down. Traps on rivers and creeks used different ways to make the water levels rise and fall to catch fish and eels.

Fish traps at Brewarrina, NSW.

TREE SCARS: Old trees show where bark has been stripped for building canoes, and making shields, dishes and boomerangs.

GRINDING STONES: These are flat rocks with different shaped grooves in them where spears and tools were sharpened, or grass seeds ground into flour.

Grinding grooves on a rock in Kangaroo Valley, NSW.

QUARRIES: Knowing where a stone tool was made, or where ochre was mined, helps us to work out ancient Aboriginal trading routes.

Hut mounds: These mounds remain long after the huts themselves have vanished. Often there are other mounds nearby with layers of ash, or hearth stones or burnt-termite-mound ovens that can also give us clues to these people's ways of life.

Food mounds: Piles of fossilised food leftovers, such as oyster shells and fish and animal skeletons, tell us where people lived, what they ate and how they hunted.

Skeletons: Human bones with evidence of arthritis in the right elbow and shoulder show that the person probably used a spear. Ancient teeth with grooves in them tell us how people used their teeth to make thread for fish nets or baskets.

So Long, Sahul

The Ice Age had come and gone and the ancient continent of Sahul was no more. In its place was the continent of mainland Australia, the island of Tasmania, and the many other tiny islands that had once been part of a vast mainland. New deserts and coastlines and new environments had formed; new settlers had arrived, including the dingo; and new tools and ways of living had been developed.

It was a very different land from the one the first people had arrived in tens of thousands of years before.

CHAPTER 4

THE WAY THEY WERE

A thousand years ago Aboriginal life was one of the most comfortable in the world. The people who lived in Australia had more leisure and better food than most people do today. Even in the desert, two or three hours foraging by the women might get enough food to feed everyone in the group. The land was richer than any modern supermarket, with thousands of plants, animals, insects and nectars to choose from. If one source of food failed, there was still plenty of choice.

Although no-one actually tilled the soil, people still took care of plant life. The best yams were left in the ground so that the plant would keep growing. People spat fruit seeds into middens to encourage more fruit trees to grow, and diverted streams to water young trees.

They also stored food. Grass and wattle seeds were kept in skin bags, or wrapped in bundles of grass that were then coated in mud. In Central Australia one food-storage area contained seventeen huge wooden dishes that could store about a tonne of grain.

In Queensland bunya and cycad nuts were stored in trenches lined with grass and paperbark. Freshwater mussels were gathered and buried in wet sand for weeks, so they'd stay alive and fresh. Wild figs were kept in balls of dried ochre. Ant larvae could be kept for times when there wasn't much else around; and dried quandongs and bush tomatoes could be stored for long periods.

Aboriginal people also made use of 'living larders'. These were places they only visited when food was scarce elsewhere, for example during severe drought. The Finke River in Central Australia was one of these places.

How to Make a Spear

9. Smear some of the resin in the notch and some on your blade.
10. Let it dry until its' tacky, then warm the blade and notch over the fire.
11. While still warm, tie the blade and barb together with a wet sinew.
(As the sinew dries it will get tighter.)
12. Wet the join with spit, then smear it with earth.
13. Leave it overnight, then heat again so that the resin softens and spreads through the sinews.
14. Keep heating and adding more resin and sinew until it's firm.
15. Keep straightening the warmed spear until it's perfectly straight.
16. Trim off any bumps and sharpen the blade.
Ouch!
17.
... and keep repeating everything over and over until it's perfect.

Awesome Art

For years Europeans thought Aboriginal art was primitive and worthless, but now the works of traditional Aboriginal artists sell for hundreds of thousands of dollars.

Some of the world's earliest art comes from Australia. Each region had its own style. The Kimberleys had their magnificent and mysterious Wanjina series (also known as the Bradshaws after the European who first wrote about them). Cape York had enormous figures of birds, plants and ancestral beings. In southern Queensland hands, axes, boomerangs and other items were held against pale stone walls and red, yellow or black pigment was stencilled around them.

Most ancient art that we know of today is rock art which has been protected from sun and rain in caves and under overhangs of rock. Bark paintings don't last long, and ceremonial didgeridoos, with their intricate decorations, were often destroyed at the end of a ceremony.

Pretty Things

Many people wore bright headbands. Many also wore belts of feather or fur or plant-fibre string, woven or plaited or fringed, and coloured with plant dyes or ochre. Bangles, necklaces and other ornaments were made of coloured seeds, clay, bones, feathers, plaited pandanus leaves, plaited or woven fibres and, especially, shells.

Fun and Games

Dolls were made of wood, shells or clay, and could be dressed in fibre skirts or feathers.

Balls were made from dried grass tied up with string, possum skin, clay, paperbark or plaited pandanus-leaf.

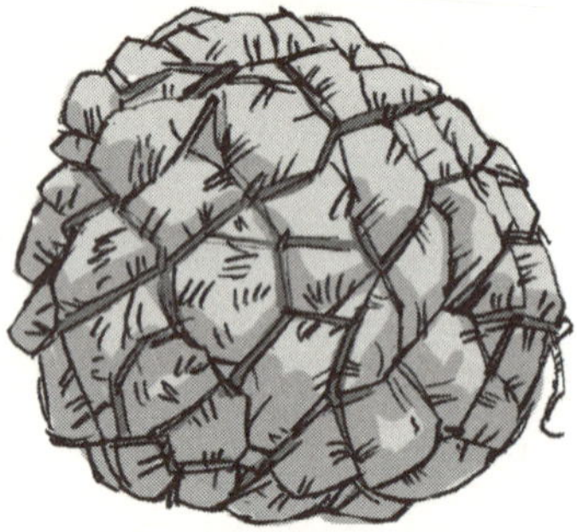

Children in the Torres Strait Islands played with toy canoes.

Adults played ball games too. Some of these games were a bit like hockey, where they hit balls with sticks.

Another ball game was like bowls, using granite balls.
Both children and adults used vines for skipping ropes. The old men of the Jawalarai people of the Narran River, NSW, were said to be the best skippers of all. They would pretend to pick thorns out of their feet, or hunt for ants, or collect grass seed or dance and jump like a frog - all while skipping.
Want a skip?
I'll skip this one.
Children made spinning tops out of wood and beeswax or hard sap.
They made pandanus-leaf birds that whirled through the air.
They pretended to gather, hunt and cook food.
They played marbles.
The marbles were made of clay, stone nuts or shells.
The Gugada children of South Australia had wooden marbles.
And like children everywhere, Aboriginal children played house and chasing games.

Digging the Dirt

Stone for tools and ochre for art and ceremonies were mined in many places across Australia. The giant flint mine at Koonalda Cave in South Australia is about seventy-five metres deep and three hundred metres long.

The Wilgie Mia red-and-yellow ochre mine in the Murchison district of Western Australia is thirty metres wide and twenty metres deep. The men hammered at the rock with stone mauls, then used fire-hardened wedges to pry out the ochre. They used scaffolding to get to the difficult areas. Ochres from Wilgie Mia were traded as far away as Queensland.

The ancient Rumbalara ochre mine, two hundred kilometres from Alice Springs, was used to make camouflage paint during World War Two.

At the Mount Roland mine in Tasmania the women were the miners.

Shopping and Swapping

Aboriginal goods were traded right across Australia, although it's not likely that any one person crossed the entire country to carry out trade. Instead, neighbouring groups exchanged valuable objects, such as special tools, at feasts. These tools might then be passed on to other people further away. Sometimes things like shells or feathers were traded simply because they were beautiful. At other times gifts were traded to bring people together in a network of kinship.

Pearl shells from the Kimberleys turned up as far away as the South Australian coast. Baler shells from Cape York were taken as far as South Australia, Victoria and Central Australia. Stone for axes might end up eight hundred kilometres from the quarry. Australian spears were so well made that they were traded as far north as the Torres Strait Islands.

The Kabi people of the Cooloola Coast in Queensland put tree gum or beeswax in their hair so they could stick parrot or cockatoo feathers into it. The Yankunytjatjara people of Central Australia threaded gumnuts through their hair. People used white sap from vines to make white decoration spots on their skin, and the scented oil from quandong seeds as hair conditioner or to soothe rough skin.

How to Make a Soft Skin Rug

7. Ask a friend to help you pull it back and forth over the trunk of a smooth-barked tree until the skin is soft and pliable.
8. Trim off the ragged bits around the edges.
9. Sew your skins to other skins to make a cloak or rug.
It's reversible!

Firestick Farming

Fire was important. It was needed for both cooking and warmth. But fire was also used for many other things. The smoke could be used to signal to people far away. Fire could heat water to make steam that helped people when they were ill, and was used to prepare medicinal plants. It hardened spear points; it hardened some stones, and shattered others, so they could be shaped into tools; and it turned yellow ochre into red ochre. Fire was also used in hunting to drive animals into nets, narrow gullies or burrows.

> **Rushes were burnt to encourage new taller rushes to grow, which could then be used to make huts.**

Land that had been burnt every few years didn't have as many bushes or as much long grass. This land was quicker to travel through, and animal tracks were clearer when hunting—and it made avoiding snakes much easier.

Birds like white cockatoos came to dig up grass roots on newly burnt land. The burnt land grew soft new green grass which attracted kangaroos and wallabies, bandicoots, brush turkeys and bush rats—and they were all good to eat.

Goannas arrived to feast on animals that had been killed in the fire.

Fire was also used to look after the land. Small controlled fires—usually much smaller and more carefully tended than today's controlled burns—would remove dead grass and undergrowth so that bigger fierce bushfires were less likely to happen.

The seeds of some plants need fire to make them sprout. Other plants like ground orchids only flower after a fire—their roots are good to eat, but the tubers can only be found when the orchids are in flower.

Most importantly, small patches of fire every few years—burnt in a mosaic pattern—made the various patches of bush different. Instead of all the bushland being green at the same time, or all of it being dry, or all the wild plums fruiting at once, the people managed the bush so that various fruits and seeds were available at different times.

Land wasn't burnt every year. People had to know exactly the right time to burn—for example, if the wattle trees blossomed heavily it meant a hot dry year was coming, so more controlled burns were needed to prevent big fires the following year. Some areas were never burnt at all, especially if they had trees and plants that could be killed by fire.

The Indigenous people of Australia knew thousands of ways to read the land and the weather. For example, they knew the wet season was on its way when they heard a certain bird's call. They could also tell when a drought was on its way, and so could plan ahead to make sure there would be lots of food, no matter what happened. Modern scientific weather forecasting is only beginning to be as accurate as traditional forecasting.

People carried burning sticks and hot coals with them wherever they went so a fire could be started in each new camp.

To start a fresh fire, a hardwood stick was rubbed against a softwood stick; or else a hard boomerang was rubbed against a softwood shield. This would eventually produce a tiny spark that ignited a nest of dry grass.

CHAPTER 5

A LAND OF MANY COUNTRIES

By the time Europeans came to Australian shores, the continent was a land of about seven hundred different nations—each with their own laws, folklore and stories—and with about 250 languages. There were too many nations to describe them all here. But what follows is a little about just a few of the nations that existed in Australia in 1770 when Captain Cook arrived.

TALKING STRINE

All but three of the Australian languages came from one common language, which we call *proto-Australian*. As various groups separated over thousands of years, the words they used and the way they spoke them gradually changed until different languages evolved.

Most European languages are also descended from a single ancient language, called *Indo-European*. But being able to speak English won't help you understand Russian.

THE ARANDA PEOPLE

The Aranda people of Central Australia lived in small groups. There was no need to build houses in the hot dry climate, but they made shelters out of grass and saplings to keep off the sun and wind.

They carried what they needed on their heads and in their hands. They wore no clothes, but wore prized decorations like necklaces and headbands.

The men hunted large animals like kangaroo and emu with spears, woomeras and boomerangs. They dug pits to trap other animals, or drove them into brush-fence traps. Plants that killed fish or sent animals to sleep were placed in waterholes—the fish were then easy to collect, and the animals that had drunk the water were slower moving and easier to hunt.

The women collected most of the food—fruits, seeds to grind into flour for cakes, roots, ant larvae, witchetty grubs, lizards and snakes. They hunted with digging sticks and collected their catches and finds in wooden dishes.

Food was shared. Eating what you had found without sharing it with others was seen as selfish and greedy.

Growing Up

When children reached puberty they underwent initiation practices involving hunger, thirst, fear and exhaustion to prove they had the courage and determination to take on adult responsibilities. For example, they had to endure agonising circumcision and cuts across the chest. After those first tests there were further initiations that continued throughout a person's life, but people could only undergo these later initiations if the elders approved and thought the person was worthy. Only outstanding people ever received the whole of their ancestors' secrets.

MAROONED!

People crossed to Tasmania about 35 000 years ago, walking across the land bridge that is now covered by Bass Strait. About twelve thousand years ago the waters of Bass Strait began to close over this bridge, and by eight thousand years ago Tasmania was cut off.

Tasmanian tools were originally the same chunky stone implements that were used on the mainland. But over the next ten thousand years Tasmanian tools became smaller and more efficient than the bigger all-purpose tools of the earlier settlers. However, the handles that were used on the mainland were never developed in Tasmania.

TASMANIAN MYSTERIES

Why didn't Tasmanians stitch their clothes? Or eat fish? Did they just prefer fat-rich foods like seals, shellfish and abalone? The early Tasmanians were excellent artists, but in the last ten thousand years they made very little art. No-one knows why.

About four thousand years ago people in Tasmania developed boats made of bundles of bark. There were no paddles—the boats were pushed by swimmers or punted with long poles in shallow water. These boats soon got waterlogged and couldn't be taken more than about fifteen kilometres out to sea. But the people made astounding voyages through rough seas and high winds to the Bass Strait islands to hunt seals or mutton birds, or to gather seabird eggs from the Maatsuyker Islands off the south coast of Tasmania.

People tended to move about and camp close to food sources or mines. But they also spent about a quarter of each year in small villages of dome-shaped huts, thatched with bark, grass or turf and lined inside with bark, skins or feathers.

Women's Work is Never Done

Women in Tasmania did almost all the work. They built the huts; mined ochre, and mined rock for tools; hunted possums for food and skins; carried the spears, game and babies; wove baskets of rushes or grasses; made shell necklaces—and gathered most of the food.

Many of the men couldn't swim, but the women were extraordinary swimmers. They dived for shellfish, and stayed underwater for long periods of time, and could swim as far as two kilometres through rough seas to go after mutton birds and their eggs. The ocean around Tasmania is often freezing, so the women rubbed themselves with a mix of mutton bird fat and red ochre to keep out the cold.

THE NYUNGAR

One of the earliest camp sites in Australia is in the territory of the Nyungar people of south-west Western Australia. The camp site is about forty thousand years old.

Even though the rest of Australia dried up during the ice age—and mostly stayed dry after that—this area stayed fertile. The people wore kangaroo-skin cloaks, possum-skin belts, and feather necklaces. They carried smouldering banksia cones, wrapped in thick skins, under their clothes to warm them in winter. Many of their tools were unique to the area—like long-handled serrated knives, and saws made of small flakes of quartz fastened with resin along lengths of wood.

The south of Western Australia has lots of shell middens, rock shelters, ochre and stone quarries, and extraordinary fish traps. The stone walls of the Oyster Harbour fish trap are about a kilometre long. Fish swam into the traps at high tide. When the tide went out the fish were stranded and could be speared, netted or caught by hand.

Ancient Surfers Paradise

People of the Durrubul, Guwar, Njula, Quandamooka, Noonuccal, Kombumeri, and Yugambeh language groups lived in the regions around south-east Queensland for at least twenty thousand years. But they were possibly there for longer than that, as older sites may be hidden under the waters of Moreton Bay.

In winter huge groups met to hunt the sea mullet in Moreton Bay. In summer people came from as far away as the Bundaberg region or the Tweed River to feast on bunya nuts in the Bunya Mountains. People traded at the feasts for possum-skin rugs, woven bags, jewellery, shells, tools and weapons. Marriages were arranged and ceremonies performed.

The cycad harvest was another great event. Cycads had to be carefully washed and cooked to get rid of their poison.

Ngunawal, Nagarigo and Wolgal

The region around present-day Canberra was once a place where various groups came together for meetings. There was once far more food growing in the Canberra region than there is now—sheep have eaten the yam daisies that once covered the hills, and other fruits such as native cherry and emu berries have vanished too. There was once a red-and-yellow ochre quarry on Red Hill, which is now a suburb of Canberra. The ochre was traded for tools and other goods.

Winters were cold and the people who lived in the area built solid huts made of logs and branches, with roofs and walls of big sheets of stringy-bark. Their cloaks were made of as many as eighty possum skins sewn together with kangaroo-leg sinew.

In summer the people moved to different places to hunt, or to attend the rich bogong-moth feasts at places like Jindabyne, Gudgenby or Omeo. Scouts travelled into the mountains and sent smoke signals when the moths arrived. About five hundred people from different tribes travelled hundreds of kilometres to feast on the moths, and to arrange marriages and conduct corroborees and initiation rites.

How to Roast Moths

THE EEL FARMERS

The biggest villages in Australia belonged to the Gunditjmara people of the Lake Condah area in Western Victoria. One of these villages might contain hundreds of huts. Each house had stone walls to about a metre high, covered with a frame of branches with bark or rush roofs. Every doorway faced the same way.

The Gunditjmara people built more than seventy-five square kilometres of artificial ponds for farming eels. Some fish traps were made of walls a metre high and fifty metres long, and were built from blocks of black rock. These walls diverted water through the marshes. Other fish-trap channels were more than thirty kilometres long. Smoking-trees were used to smoke and preserve the eels for export to other parts of Australia. These eel farms were so big and efficient that they fed up to ten thousand people.

Central Victoria had several greenstone quarries. This hard volcanic rock could be flaked into chips and then ground to a hard sharp edge. These blades were as sharp as modern knives and often stayed sharper for longer.

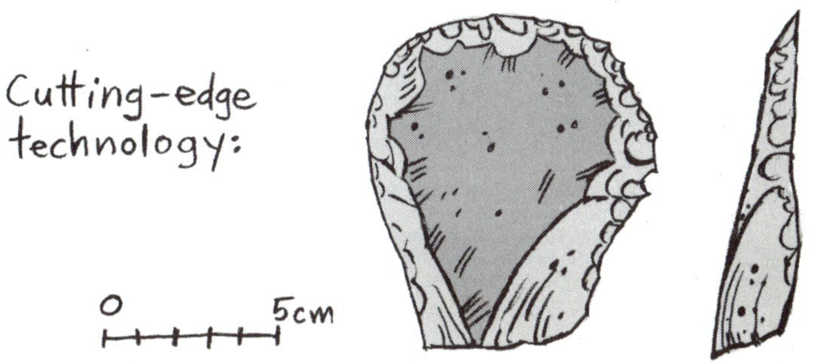

People traded greenstone tools for weapons, belts, possum-skin rugs and cloaks, necklaces and ornaments. These tools have been discovered more than three hundred kilometres from the mines, and were probably traded with people who had marriage ties or other social links with the miners.

Aussie Rules Rule

Australian Rules football was possibly invented in the Western Districts of Victoria, long before white people arrived. The early game was played with possum-skin balls, and the players made the same spectacular leaps to catch the ball (take a mark). Some say Aussie Rules comes from Gaelic Football in Ireland—but Gaelic Football doesn't include this form of mark-taking.

Harbour Views

The Cadigal people lived on the southern side of Port Jackson and along the Cooks River. Around Botany Bay were the Dharawal, and their country comprised all of modern-day Sutherland Shire as well as Wollongong. The Guringai people occupied the northern side of Port Jackson and around Broken Bay, while the Bidjigal lived further west in places like Parramatta and Castle Hill.

We know more about the way of life of the people who lived around Sydney Harbour than any other group. This was because some of the early British settlers, such as Watkin Tench, kept diaries of what they observed.

The Cadigal lived in small round huts with domed roofs made of a framework of saplings. Inside were possum, platypus, kangaroo, wallaby, or glider-skin rugs. Women made wood and bark carry-dishes and water containers, waterproofed with grass-tree sap or eucalypt resin.

Watkin Tench (1758–1833)

Watkin Tench came to New Holland, as Australia was then known, as a captain of marines on the First Fleet in 1788. He vividly described all he saw in the colony, and also found out as much as he could about the Aboriginal people. After a life of many military adventures he retired as a lieutenant general and adopted his brother's four orphaned children, as he and his wife had no children of their own.

Sydney Supermarket

Wild fruit grew everywhere—cherries, geebungs, billardiera, Port Jackson figs—and the fruit was eaten fresh or made into dried sweets. The roots of yam daisies were baked in hot ashes, and were also ground to flour and made into flat cakes. Bracken roots were eaten too, as were many orchids and lily-roots.

Blossoms, or honey from wild bees, were soaked in water to make a sweet drink.

Fish were plentiful for most of the year. Men speared them from the rocks or in the shallows along the beach, using spears up to four metres long made from wattle branches or the dried flower-stems of grass trees. Women fished from canoes on the harbour. Their handlines were spun from the inner bark of the kurrajong tree, then soaked in bloodwood sap to stop them fraying or rotting in the salt water. Fish were also netted, as well as caught in giant fish traps.

A young man might give a girl a present of fishing hooks and lines.

Canoes were made from stringy-bark or casuarina bark stripped off the tree in large sheets with stone axes, then bunched at each end and tied with vines or woven cord. They were about four metres long and could be made in a day. The canoes sat low in the water—so low that from a distance it looked like the occupant was sitting *on* the water. The canoes could carry up to five people, often for long distances up and down the coast. The women sang and gossiped, holding their children between their knees to leave their hands free to paddle or fish. They chewed cockles and mussels and spat them into the water to attract the fish. A small fire on a bed of seaweed, sand or clay on the bottom of the canoe was kept burning to cook fish as they were caught, but most of the catch was brought ashore to be shared.

Oil was squeezed out of the fish guts and used to keep off mosquitoes and sandflies, and was possibly rubbed on the skin to keep warm while diving.

Men and women gathered shellfish along the shore and netted lobsters. A beached whale was the signal for a feast. Whales were cut into chunks and lightly cooked. Dolphins were prepared the same way.

Babies were wrapped in paperbark sheets. Paperbark is both soft and waterproof. People also made cloaks of beaten paperbark fibre.

Each spring there was an eel feast in what is now the Parramatta area, with people travelling from far away to take part. The eels were caught in traps made of two long hollow pieces of wood joined together. The eels sheltered in the traps and were easily pulled out before they had a chance to escape. Summer was the time for great fish feasts and initiations, where men and women were painted with white clay.

Land of Lost Nations

When Europeans arrived on the shores of New Holland, the continent was a land of many countries. People sang the songs only of their own particular country. They didn't tell the stories of another people's country, or burn another people's country, or hunt in another people's country. They didn't steal land, or sell it, or give it away.

In the early years of white settlement the Aboriginal people were forcibly moved off their traditional lands and onto land they didn't know. In the process they lost not just their country, but their history as well.

For a long time Australia had been isolated from the great technological changes of the outside world, especially in Asia and Europe. Now that outside world was coming to Australia.

CHAPTER 6

DISCOVERED—AGAIN AND AGAIN!

For most Europeans, the only good reason to sail south was to find gold or spices, and the only interesting place in the South Pacific was the Spice Islands—now called Indonesia—with its nutmeg, cloves, mace, pepper and cinnamon. During the past thousand years Chinese, Javanese, Indian, Japanese, Cambodian and Siamese merchants have all been part of the spice trade, and spices were traded by several routes to countries in Europe.

Traders knew that a great south land, *Terra Australis*, existed somewhere to the south of the Spice Islands. No-one knew how big the land was, but there were rumours that it was very large—and that it wasn't just a map-maker's way of filling in the ocean with something other than whales, mermaids and dragons. Even the earliest world map we know of, made by Ptolemy of Alexandria 2200 years ago, shows a great southern continent.

There were also rumours that this southern land was a land of gold.

THE GREAT CHINESE FLEET

The Chinese may have been among the first people in historic times to visit the Australian continent. By the 500s CE they already knew of a land where men threw boomerangs and animals hopped on their hind legs. By the 1400s Chinese maps included a land called Greater Java, which they showed sitting below Java itself. This Greater Java may have been the northern coast of Australia.

By 1403 China had become the most powerful nation in the world. The new Chinese emperor Yongle (or Yung-Lo) had an army of more than one million men armed with guns, and a navy of more than a hundred giant ships, each capable of carrying over two thousand tonnes of cargo. The biggest cargo fleet in Europe at that time was an Italian fleet based in Venice, and it had only three hundred ships, the largest of which was capable of carrying only fifty tonnes of cargo.

The Grand Eunuch Zheng He was appointed Commander-in-Chief of the world's largest fleet.

THE THREE-JEWELLED EUNUCH

Men who had their penis and testicles removed were called *eunuchs*. They were subjected to this operation so that they would be unable to father children. This meant they would remain loyal to their masters, instead of seeking riches, power or status to pass on to their offspring. Zheng He kept his penis and testicles—his three jewels—in a tiny jewelled casket that he wore under his cloak. He wanted to be buried with them, so that in the next life he would be a whole man again.

Chinese Down-under

In 1421 four massive Chinese fleets set sail to every corner of the world. The Chinese emperor's aim was to collect tribute from the barbarians and to bring Confucian harmony to the earth, as well as to explore for minerals and collect new plants for medicine and food.

Ships from these four fleets explored more of the world than explorers from any other country would for centuries to come. They almost certainly reached South America and Antarctica. It is also likely that they reached Australia, but most of the records of these voyages and of Yongle's reign were destroyed when the emperor was driven from power.

Mysterious Great South Land

The earliest European map that shows something a bit like Australia was drawn in 1542 by Jean Rotz, who made maps for King Henry VIII of England. French maps made between 1540 and 1570 show a place called *Java la Grande* south-east of Sumatra. They also show another mysterious land further to the south which they sometimes called *Terra Australis Incognita*, which is Latin for *unknown southern land*. This giant land went all the way down to the Antarctic, and was drawn further east than where Australia really is.

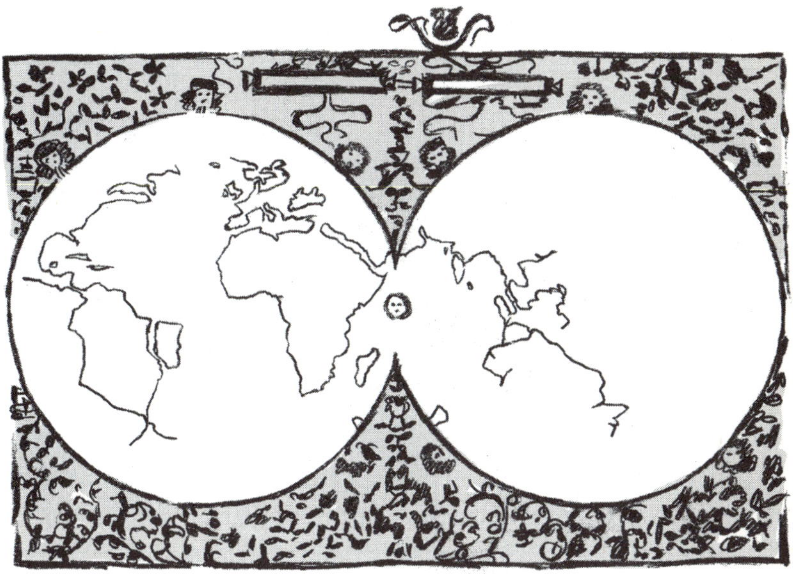

The Portuguese Pop By

In 1493 Pope Alexander VI divided the world in two—one half for Spain, the other half for Portugal—because he believed he had the right to give away any lands where heathen people lived. This meant he gave away Australia, too—even though he probably didn't know it.

The Portuguese quickly spread into their half of the world. By the 1520s they had discovered the route—via Cape Town—to Ambon in the Moluccas and to the Spice Islands, and they had even sailed east of Timor. This meant their ships were close to Australia—so close that a storm could have blown them onto the Australian coast—and so close that the sailors would have been able to see the smoke from fires on the shore.

The Portuguese probably landed on Australia, even though we have no record of it. Perhaps the 'danger coast' shown on Portuguese maps of Greater Java referred to the rocks and reefs of the Great Barrier Reef. Perhaps Cristovao de Mendonca landed on the Australian coast in 1522 when he searched for the Isles of Gold beyond Sumatra. Maybe Gomes de Sequeira found Australia when he was blown off-course in 1525.

Perhaps there are no records of these landings because the Portuguese Government didn't want other countries to know about Australia—in case it had spices or riches that other countries would take. Or maybe—like most other visitors to Australia before 1770—they simply decided that Australia was not worth bothering about.

The Mahogany Mystery

Among the many shipwrecks along the south-west coast of modern-day Victoria—known as *shipwreck coast*—is the Mahogany Ship. It was first made famous by a conman, Hugh Donnelly, who claimed to have seen it when his own boat sank in 1836. But Donnelly didn't arrive in Victoria until 1841.

The ship was first reliably described by Captain John Mills in 1836. He said it had 'hard dark timber, like mahogany'. Many others have claimed to have seen it—in the ocean, or in the sand dunes. Some said it was a fifty-tonne ship, and others that it was three hundred tonnes. At least some of the stories about the Mahogany Ship have been fakes or fiction. The last sighting of its mysterious dark timbers was during the 1880s.

Some people say the Mahogany Ship was Portuguese, perhaps the ship captained by Cristovao de Mendonca which was lost in the early 1500s. Others say it was a Chinese wreck. Still others say it is just another whaler or sealing vessel, one of many wrecked along that coast.

In 1992 the Victorian Government posted a reward of a quarter of a million dollars for anyone who could find it. No-one has successfully claimed the money yet.

Spanish Treasure-hunters

The Spanish were the first Europeans we definitely know to have sailed into the Pacific Ocean. They were hunting for gold. Pedro Fernándes de Quirós was sent out in 1605 specifically to find the Great South Land and claim it—and its gold—for Spain. Instead he found what is now called the New Hebrides. He called it *Austrialia del Espiritu Santo*.

Unfortunately for de Quirós, the New Hebrideans didn't agree with him about becoming Spanish. De Quirós and his men were driven off. But his journey helped to fuel the rumour that the rich land of *Terra Australis Incognita* was down there—somewhere.

One of the ships in de Quirós' expedition passed through the strait between Papua New Guinea and Australia. That strait now bears the name of the ship's captain, Luis Váez de Torres. It is called the Torres Strait.

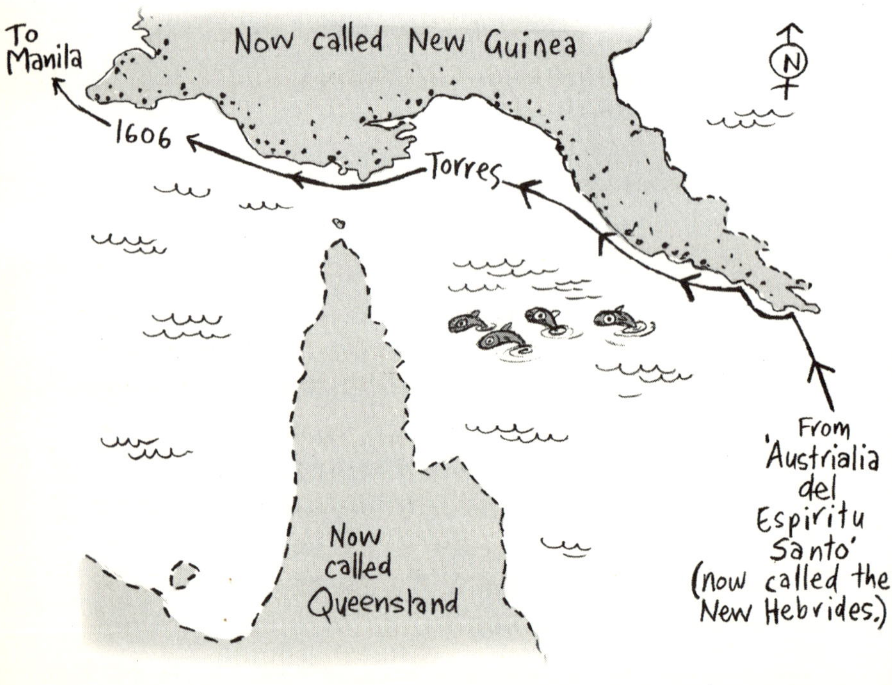

Those Marvellous Maps!

More than a hundred years later a Scotsman, Alexander Dalrymple, dreamed of finding the Great South Land.

Alexander Dalrymple

He had studied the old Spanish maps, and he gave Sir Joseph Banks—the English scientist who later accompanied James Cook on the voyage of the *Endeavour*—copies of two maps that showed de Torres' strait. Sir Joseph later showed these maps to Cook.

It was the maps of this strait that tempted Cook to reach the Indian Ocean by travelling around the north of Australia instead of sailing via the south of Tasmania. If Cook had never made that east-coast voyage, he might never have stopped at Botany Bay, and there might never have been a settlement at Port Jackson. Without de Torres and his map, Australian history might have been very different.

Visitors? What Visitors?

In all this time, of course, the actual inhabitants of Australia had no idea that others were daydreaming about the possible riches of their land. Even if the Chinese, Spanish or Portuguese had landed on Australian shores, they soon went away again, and most of the local inhabitants never knew they had even visited.

Batavia - 1774

CHAPTER 7

ACCIDENTAL TOURISTS

The Dutch weren't impressed by the Pope's gift of half the world to the Portuguese, especially when that half contained the Spice Islands. Fortunately for the Dutch, Spain annexed Portugal in 1580, and Spain was too busy looking after its vast empire in the Americas to be able to look after the Spice Islands as well. In 1602 the Dutch East India Company was formed. It took the Portuguese fort at Ambon in 1605 and eventually made its headquarters at Jakarta, which they renamed Batavia. For the next two hundred years the Dutch East India Company dominated the spice trade.

Willem Wanders In

In 1605–1606 the Dutch captain Willem Janszoon sailed east from the Spice Islands in the *Duyfken* on a voyage of exploration. He entered the Gulf of Carpentaria, but he thought that the land he saw was the coast of New Guinea. Without realising it, Janszoon then charted three hundred kilometres of the northern Australian coast.

The Dutch wanted to find a route from Batavia, past New Guinea and through to the Pacific Ocean, so they could avoid sailing too close to the Spanish in the Philippines. (Of course, de Torres had already found a way, but the Spanish had kept this a secret from the Dutch).

What Gulf is This, Anyway?

In 1623 two Dutch ships, the *Pera* and *Arnhem*, sailed from the island of Ambon under the command of Captain Willem van Colster and Captain Jan Cartenszoon. They charted the Gulf of Carpentaria and the coast of what is now known as Arnhem Land, and nailed a board up on a tree on an uninhabited sandy island in the Gulf of Carpentaria to show that the Dutch had claimed the land. They also kidnapped a Cape York man.

But just like Janszoon before them, they too thought the gulf was part of New Guinea, though they did notice that the Cape York people looked very different from the people of

New Guinea. They didn't think much of the country either. Cartenszoon said there were no fruit-bearing trees, or anything that a person could make use of. Where was the gold? Where were the spices? According to him it was the most arid and barren region that could be found on earth.

In 1636 Pieter Pieterszoon also assumed that the north of Australia was part of New Guinea.

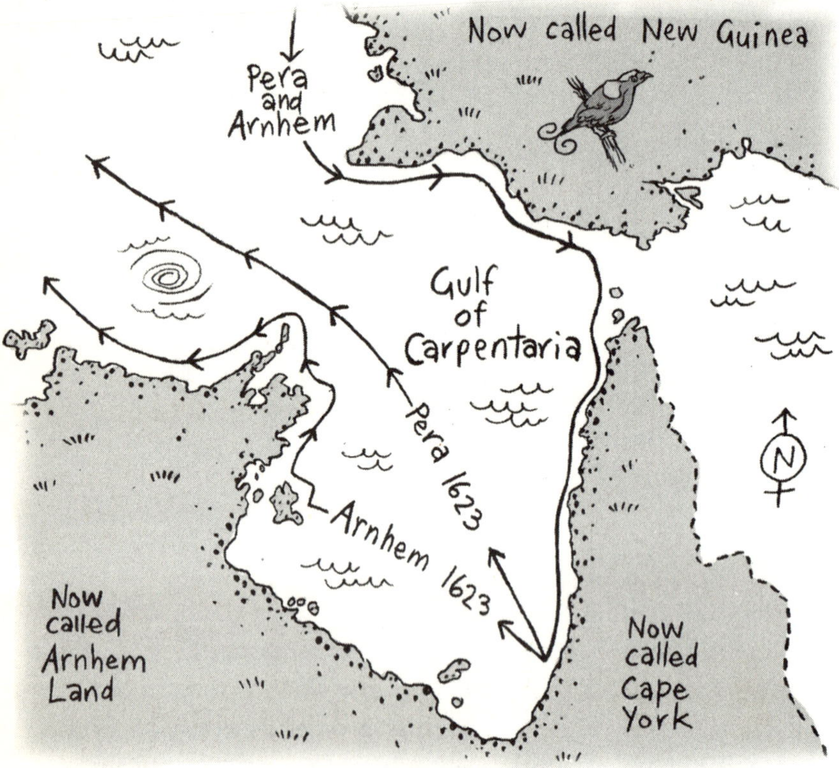

European explorers now had a pretty good idea of what the northern coast of Australia looked like—even though they still didn't know how big the rest of the country was. Western Australia was next to be mapped—but this time, the discovery of the coastline happened mostly by accident.

WHERE'S THE DUNNY?

When at sea, most sailors were either constipated or had the runs. The captain and important passengers had chamber pots which were kept in a cupboard and were emptied by their servants. Most of the sailors either aimed over the side for Number Ones (the crew were all men) or sat on a seat suspended over the ocean at the bow of the ship for Number Twos—a bit breezy on the bum, but no-one had to worry about the plumbing. There was no toilet paper. People rinsed themselves from a bucket of sea water kept nearby. Or else they wiped their bums with a frayed knot that dangled from the end of a rope into the sea.

Getting out of the Doldrums

The most direct route from Holland to the Spice Islands was via the Atlantic Ocean, south of the Cape of Good Hope, then across the Indian Ocean from Madagascar to Java. But the ships were often becalmed near the equator—in the doldrums—which means they had no wind to fill the sails, leaving them stranded.

In 1611 a Dutch captain accidentally discovered how to avoid the doldrums. After rounding the Cape,

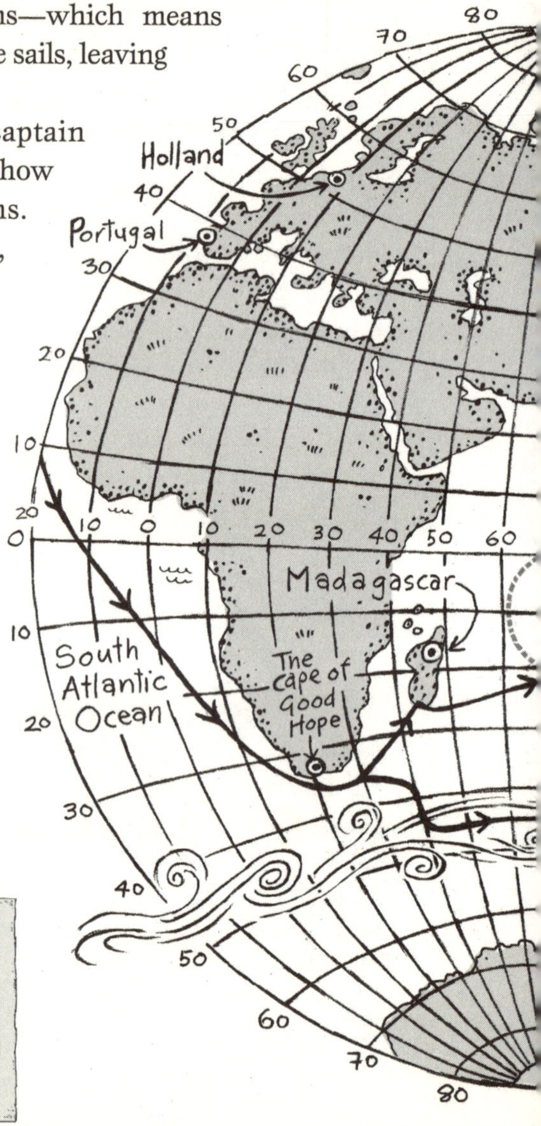

These trade winds are also called the Roaring Forties, because they are between the latitudes of 40 and 50 degrees south.

he made a dogleg at about 40 degrees south, then used the strong westerly trade winds in the south-east Indian ocean to push the ship east for about three thousand kilometres before turning north towards Java.

Without wind, a sailing ship can neither move nor change course. Even if waves are driving the ship against rocks, the sailors can do nothing about it. Ships that were becalmed in the doldrums could be stranded for months, far from fresh food and water. Entire crews died of heat and thirst.

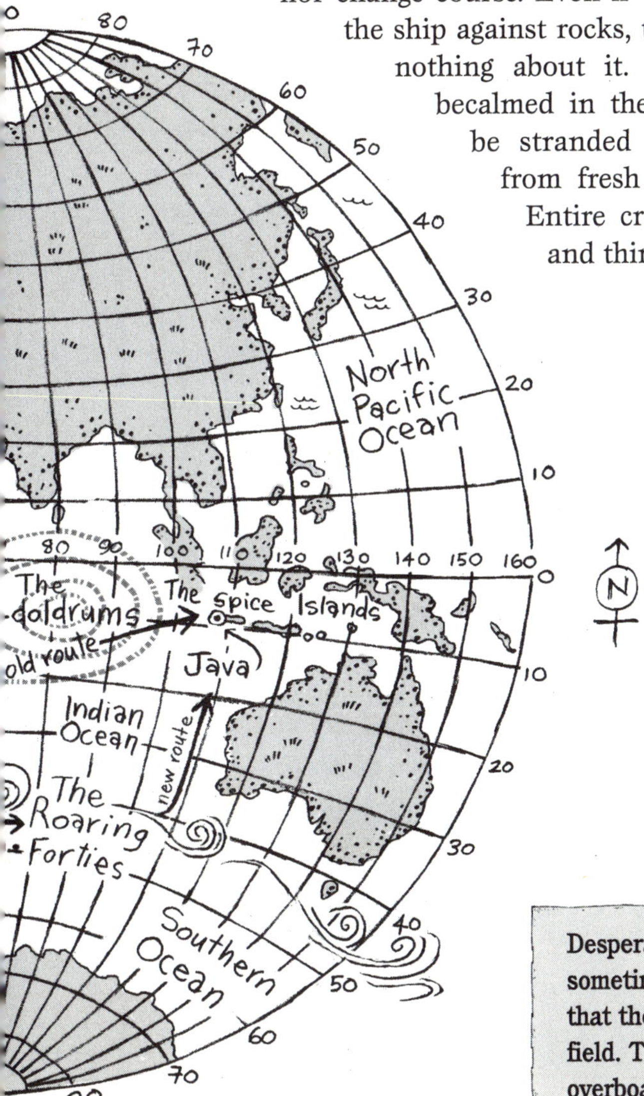

Desperate sailors would sometimes hallucinate that the sea was a green field. They would step overboard—and drown.

The Problem of Longitude

One of the great problems for sailors before the mid-1700s was working out exactly where they were once the land was out of sight. It was fairly easy to work out which direction to go—they followed the stars or the sun. But it was impossible to work out exactly how far they had travelled.

There are two sets of lines drawn on maps—lines of *latitude* (going across the map) and *longitude* (which go from top to bottom). Of course these lines don't occur on the actual sea or land, but are used on maps as guides to location.

Latitude was fairly simple for sailors to calculate—they could work out where they were by measuring the length of the day; or the height of the sun above the horizon; or the height of

certain stars above the horizon. But to measure longitude they needed to know two things: the time on board ship as *well* as the time at another place of known longitude at the very same moment.

Before the invention of clocks that kept accurate time, sailors couldn't use this method. They could work out the time where they were . . . but how would they know what time it was half a world away? Navigators often miscalculated their position so badly that they ended up lost at sea or shipwrecked.

In 1761 an English clockmaker, John Harrison, perfected a clock that could keep the true time of the home port, despite the rolling of the ship and extremes of weather. The problem of calculating longitude was solved.

Dirk Was Here

There was no accurate way for ship's masters to work out how strong the trade winds were, how fast those winds were carrying them, or how far east the winds had blown them.

Only five years after the new route to the Spice Islands was discovered in 1611, a Dutch captain sailed too far east before turning north, and came across the western coast of Australia. Maybe others had done the same thing before him—but they left no record of it.

This captain, however, left proof that he had landed. Captain Dirk Hartog erected a post on a small island off the coast near Shark Bay, and nailed an inscribed pewter plate onto it, proclaiming that his ship, the *Eendracht*, had landed there on 25 October 1616. This is the first written evidence of a European landing in Australia.

Hartog sailed the *Eendracht* back to Java after naming the land *Eendrachtsland* after his ship—in other words, *Land of Concord.*

Exploring New Holland May 1618

Captain Haevik Claeszoon Van Hillegom in the ship 'Zeewolf' sighted the west coast of Australia in the vicinity of North West Cape.

July 1618

A couple of months later Captain Lenaert Jacobszoon saw the same part of the coast from the 'Mauritus'.

1619

Frederik de Houtman, in the 'Dordrecht', sailed up the west coast from around Fremantle. On his way he came across some islands and named them after himself – Houtman's Abrolhos. (Abrolhos is Portuguese for 'keep your eyes open!')

1621 – 1622

The ship 'Leeuwin', captained by an unknown Dutchman, rounded the south-west cape that still bears its name. The sailors saw that the coastline ran towards the east.

The English ship *Tryall* was Australia's first recorded shipwreck. It ran onto a reef near the Montebello Islands in 1622. Forty-five people managed to get to Batavia in the ship's boats, but a further ninety-three people were abandoned with the wreck and left to perish.

In 1627 Francois Thijszoon and Pieter Nuyts' ship *t'Gulden Zeepaerdt* was separated from its fleet. They, too, rounded Cape Leeuwin, then travelled east along the southern coast of the continent and mapped it for about a thousand kilometres. But neither the *Leeuwin* nor *t'Gulden Zeepaerdt* landed along the coast. Nothing on what they were now calling *Terra Australis Cognita*—or *Known South Land*—attracted the explorers to the shore.

How to Make *Dunderfunk*, or 'Thunder and Lightning' (a specialty on Dutch ships)

MAGGOTS ON THE SIDE

Most stored food in the seventeenth century was either dried or salted, and it rotted in the damp. Ships were pretty damp, so only food that was stored in barrels of vinegar or brine survived for the months or years that a ship might spend at sea. But barrels were bulky and heavy, and the ships were already loaded with men, sails, rigging, cargo, guns and ammunition. Naval ships needed to be fast, and cargo ships needed room for cargo. Food for the sailors was the first thing to be cut back on—especially if it was in heavy barrels.

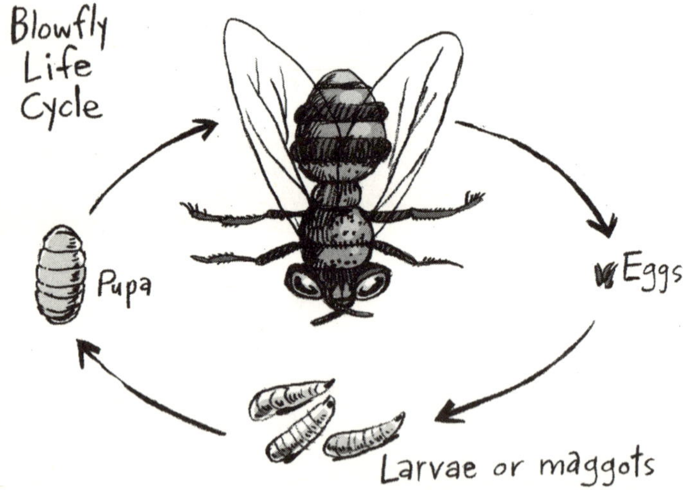

Food that was stored on board a ship included salted fish, hard cheese, rice, peas, oatmeal, kegs of salted butter, vinegar and pickled vegetables. Live pigs, sheep and even cows were also kept on board so that there would be fresh food for as long as possible—and then there was the hay for all the animals.

Officers and important guests brought their own food to complement the ship's basic supplies. No ship's stores were ever thrown away, no matter how old or bad they got, except for rotten cheese. Ship's biscuit might be forty years old before it even came aboard!

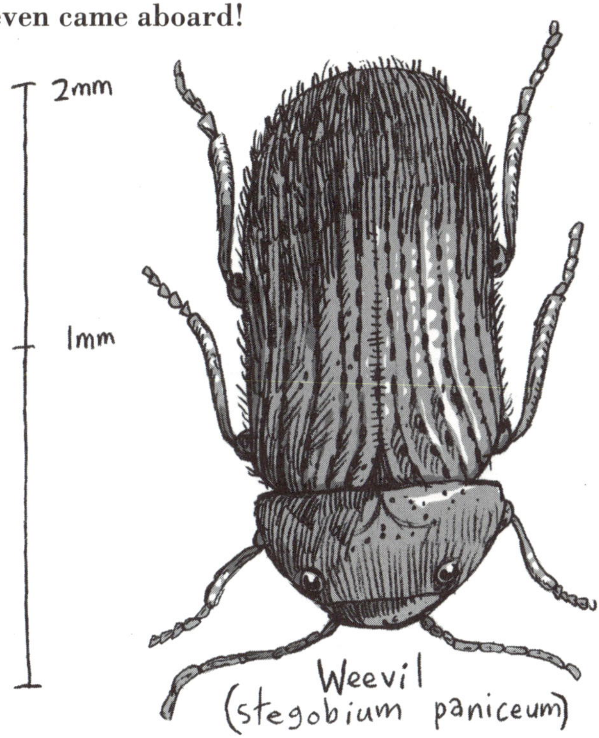

Fresh food soon ran out. The sailors ate so much salty food that their lips and tongues were burned and blistered. Fresh water was scarce and often so old that it stank. Water was mixed with wine or rum, which helped to kill the bacteria, or else brewed into ale. Sailors' only hot drink was a mix of beer, brandy or rum, sweetened with sugar and warmed with an iron rod heated over the galley fire.

The Wreck of the *Batavia*

Commander François Pelsaert was another Dutchman who discovered a part of Australia by accident. He was on his way from Holland to the Spice Islands, with a cargo of treasure. On board were some men who were plotting to take over the ship and become pirates. But on 4 June 1629 the ship, the *Batavia*, was wrecked on a reef off the Houtman Abrolhos Islands.

Some of the 316 passengers, crew and soldiers drowned, but 268 survivors managed to reach the nearby islands. The shipwrecked people hunted desperately for fresh water, but couldn't find any. They survived by drinking from rain puddles on the rocks. There were so many flies that it was impossible to keep them out of their mouths and eyes.

The survivors twice met Aboriginal people, whom Pelsaert described as 'black savages, quite naked'. In a cold country like Holland even the poorest people wore clothes—so for Pelsaert it followed that those who had no clothes at all must be 'savages'. It never occurred to Pelsaert that these so-called savages had a highly developed understanding of the bare and barren islands he had been shipwrecked on.

Blood on the Island

Leaving the passengers and most of the crew behind, Commander François Pelsaert and forty-seven people from the wrecked ship set off for Java in two small sailing boats to find help.

They had no fresh water and few supplies. One of the boats had to be abandoned and they were rescued thirty-three days later—with no loss of life—by the ship *Frederik Hendrik* in the Sunda Strait between Sumatra and Java. They had travelled more than two thousand kilometres. It was an incredible feat of seamanship and navigation.

While Pelsaert was away the mutinous band, led by Jeronimus Corneliszoon, planned to seize the rescue boat when it returned and continue with their plans to become pirates. Water was in desperately short supply, and some people died of thirst. The mutineers sent some of the people who were not part of their plot to other islands to search for water, and then killed 125 of the men, women and children who were left behind, by clubbing, stabbing and drowning them.

The group of people who had gone to find water built two small stone huts or forts to protect themselves from the mutineers while they waited for rescue. The foundations of these still remain on West Wallabi Island. They were probably the first European houses ever built in Australia.

That September Pelsaert returned in a ship called the *Sardam*. The loyal band of survivors, who had remained on West Wallabi Island, warned Pelsaert of the mutiny, and Pelsaert managed to capture the mutineers. He hanged some of them on the spot, and took others back to Batavia to be hanged there. Two of them were marooned on the coast of Western Australia.

To *maroon* someone is to punish them by leaving them behind on a desolate island or piece of coastline. Marooned sailors were not expected to survive.

The rest of the mutineers were either flogged or *keelhauled*—which involved being dragged by a rope under the ship, from one side to the other, and was an agonising and terrifying way to die. It was even more agonising to survive being keelhauled.

Not Worth the Trouble

The Dutch had claimed Australia. But they didn't follow up their claim by establishing a settlement, which was what you had to do in those days to really claim a land. To the Dutch, the land looked dry and forbidding. There were few safe harbours or river mouths where a sailing ship could shelter from storms. Furthermore, the spice trade, which they controlled, provided them with all the merchandise their fleet could handle—so who cared about a barren land like New Holland?

Chapter 8

The Golden Land

Europeans kept imagining that there must be a fabulous land of gold somewhere in the southern ocean. But they didn't believe that New Holland could be it. The western and northern coasts of New Holland were by now quite well-known—and people thought the coastline was really, really boring. It didn't look like a land of gold and riches at all.

The entire coast of Australia had not yet been mapped, but it was becoming clear that it was a pretty big place. So people decided that the fabulous land of gold must be further to the east, in what we now know is mostly Pacific Ocean. Dutch map-makers drew the western coast of Australia on their maps, but they continued to draw a separate mythical South Land, *Terra Australis Incognita*, far to the east.

And sailors kept searching for that land of gold.

The Land of Giants

In 1642 the Governor-General of the Spice Islands, Antonio van Diemen, sent Captain Abel Janszoon Tasman of the Dutch East India Company on a mission. Along with the talented pilot, hydrographer and surveyor, Frans Jacobszoon Visscher, Tasman sailed two ships—the *Heemskerck* and the *Zeehaen*—in search of that other really rich land they hoped existed far away to the east. Tasman was even ordered to avoid, and keep well south of, the barren land of New Holland that earlier Dutchmen had already charted.

Van Diemen hoped that Tasman would find a passage from the East Indies through to the Pacific Ocean, because he wanted the Dutch to be able to attack the Spanish settlements of South America.

ARE YOU ABLE, ABEL?

First Tasman sailed from Holland to Mauritius via the Cape of Good Hope, where he had his ships repaired. Then the two ships sailed approximately three thousand kilometres south to catch the swift trade winds. By sailing east at this latitude they would have missed the continent of New Holland altogether.

If Tasman had stayed on this course he would have reached New Zealand without ever seeing New Holland. But fierce storms in the Southern Ocean forced him to veer north, and the first land he saw was the west coast of Tasmania. Tasman thought he had made landfall on New Holland. He called the place Van Diemen's Land, after his Governor-General.

Bumping into Tassie

Tasman soon decided that Van Diemen's Land was inhabited by giants. He saw notches cut into tree trunks at least 1.5 metres apart, and thought this meant the local people were so tall they could take 1.5-metre strides. In spite of the giants supposedly lurking in the forest, Tasman raised the Dutch flag and claimed the country—again.

Governor-General Van Diemen had ordered Tasman to get the consent of local kings before claiming land for Holland. But Tasman decided that this land didn't have a king, so all he needed to do to claim it was put up a sign.

Tasman spent ten days mapping the coast of Van Diemen's Land, then continued east and crossed what is now called the Tasman Sea. There he came across the south island of New Zealand. Believing he'd found the Great South Land at last—and that he'd succeeded where others had failed—Tasman sailed back to Batavia via Tonga and the north of New Guinea.

Missing the Point

Tasman had missed a lot more than he'd found—and he misinterpreted just about everything that he *did* find. He sailed right around Australia without ever seeing the mainland; he didn't realise that Tasmania was an island; he thought he had landed on the mythical Great South Land when he'd landed on New Zealand, and he missed the Torres Strait. But Tasman *had* proved that Australia wasn't connected to Antarctica; and also that it wasn't a part of the Great South Land—because he believed that New Zealand was it. After Tasman's expedition, most maps referred to Australia as *New Holland*, recognising the Dutch claim to the land.

Tasman Tries Again

In 1644 van Diemen sent Tasman on another voyage to map the east coast of New Holland as well as to find and map the northern parts of the Great South Land he was supposed to have discovered. However, Tasman couldn't get through the reefs of Torres Strait, so instead he mapped the north and west coasts of New Holland. First he mapped the Gulf of Carpentaria; then he sailed west and south, mapping nearly five thousand miles of coastline and proving that the coast of Carpentaria joined the West Australian coast.

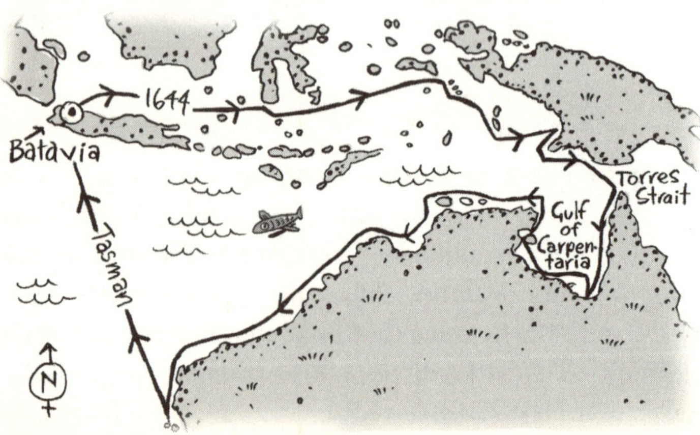

When he had finished, Tasman wrote a report saying that New Holland was worthless and that there was no profit to be made there. All he had seen were naked people walking along the beaches.

It Must Be There Somewhere!

Tasman's second voyage was a tremendous achievement—but Tasman's superiors in the Dutch East India Company didn't seem to think so. They declared that, in future, exploration should be trusted to more vigilant and courageous persons: people who would map the great land of spices and riches that they just *knew* was there. Although Tasman was in fact a brilliant explorer, captain and navigator, the Dutch East India Company thought he was simply too stupid to find the golden land. The Dutch East India Company also decided that there was no point investigating New Holland any further—it was too barren and had nothing to trade, so why bother?

Back-to-front Down-under

On the third-last day of 1696 Willem de Vlamingh (who had been looking for a missing Dutch East India Company ship) arrived with his three ships at Rottnest Island off Western Australia. He found giant rats with pouches big enough to put his fist into, as well as fragrant sandalwood trees.

De Vlamingh then sailed to the mainland and explored the Swan River. He was delighted by the white cockatoos and blue-and-green parrots.

He also captured two black swans. No European had ever seen black swans, but naturalists had predicted that swans of the southern hemisphere would have to be the opposite of the white swans of the northern hemisphere—that is, black. And they were right—for all the wrong reasons!

The country around the Swan River seemed more fertile than the land further to the north. But there was still no gold or spices—nor even fruits or grains with which to restock the ships.

After leaving the Swan River, de Vlamingh travelled up the coast and found the plate that Dirk Hartog had left there eighty years earlier. He sent it back to Holland to prove the Dutch had claimed the land, along with a watercolour painting showing where it had been found. Then he set up another plate where Hartog's had been, to show that the land still belonged to the Dutch.

Exploring New Holland

1705

Martin van Delft explored Melville Island and the Coburg Peninsula on his way to the Spice Islands.

1712

Two Dutch India Company ships were wrecked off the west coast of Australia. The 'Zuytdorp', captained by Martinus Wijsvliet, was wrecked just south of Shark Bay, on rocks at the bottom of cliffs which are now named after the ship.

1727

The 'Zeewijk', under Captain Jan Steyns, was wrecked on the Houtman Abrolhos Islands. The survivors built a boat from the wreckage, called it 'Sloepie' and sailed it to Batavia.

There was another Dutch expedition of exploration in 1756—but like all other Dutchmen who had seen New Holland, the captain and crew of this ship came to the conclusion that the coast was dry and useless.

The Mystery of the *Concordia*

In the early 1700s the Dutch ship *Concordia* was wrecked off the Western Australian coast. There is a legend that eighty men and ten women survived and made their way across the desert to found a colony, probably in Palm Valley, near what is now known as Hermannsburg, in Central Australia. However, no solid evidence for the existence of this colony has ever been found.

The Dutch weren't the only visitors to Australian shores in the early eighteenth century. By 1720 the *trepang* trade was well underway. Trepang are sea slugs, or *bêche-de-mer*, and Indonesian fishermen sailed their *praus* to northern Australia every year to spear them or catch them in nets. The trepang were then boiled, gutted, and boiled again in big pots with mangrove bark to give them a better colour and flavour. After that the slugs were dried in a smokehouse and taken back to the merchants in Macassar, most of whom were Chinese. They exported them to China (where people believed they made you feel sexy and used them in soup).

The trepang fishermen set up big camps along the Australian coast, usually in places that could be defended from attack, like promontories or small islands. They never ventured inland as the country was strongly defended by the local people. Sometimes whole camps of trepang fishermen were massacred, but at other times trade was friendly. Australian Aboriginal people are known to have travelled to Indonesia with Indonesian fishing crews.

The Final Frontier

By 1700 Australia had been mapped on three sides—the north, the west and the south. Most maps showed New Guinea as part of Australia, just as it had actually been tens of thousands of years earlier during the last ice age. Only the east coast remained unmapped. But it seemed that no-one was interested in the east. They probably thought it would be as boring as the west. Like the discovery of the west coast, the mapping of Australia's east coast would happen almost by chance.

CHAPTER 9

FACT-FINDING MISSIONS

The reasons for the early European expeditions to Australia were to look for gold or spices, or at least for slaves and profit. But in the eighteenth century people began to develop a thirst for knowledge. This was especially the case with the French and the British. They reasoned that while the unknown parts of the Pacific Ocean mightn't contain great wealth, they would surely contain new islands, people, animals and plants that might be interesting.

As early as 1666 the British Royal Society had issued directions to 'Seamen, bound for far voyages', instructing them to observe nature and build up a picture of the world.

One of the first seamen to do this was William Dampier.

The Cannibal Pirates

William Dampier was an English *privateer*. A privateer had permission from the British king or queen to plunder ships belonging to other countries, so long as he gave some of his loot to the monarch. By contrast, a *pirate* stole only for himself.

Dampier had a reputation as 'the mildest-mannered man who ever scuttled a ship or cut a throat'.

Over his career, Dampier sailed around the world three times, and he wrote detailed accounts of all that he saw. He probably provided more information about the world to more people than any person had done before.

Dampier joined a group of buccaneers in 1683 (though not for the first time!). He claimed he became a buccaneer because he was curious and wanted to see the world. He generally kept himself apart from the rest of the pirate crews on board ship, preferring to write and study. However, he also lent a hand capturing ships and committing murder.

***Buccaneer* is another word for *pirate*.**

While Dampier was on board the pirate ship *Cygnet*, the crew ran so short of food that they considered eating the officers, starting with the fat captain. Dampier himself was too skinny to make a good meal.

The *Cygnet* was blown ashore on the north-western coast of Australia in 1688. Dampier and the rest of the crew spent several weeks there while the ship was repaired, and took lots of notes about what he saw.

After many hair-raising adventures, Dampier arrived back in England in 1691, with his journals and a tattooed slave who he hoped to exhibit to make a living, but who he had to sell instead. Dampier wrote about his travels in *A New Voyage Round the World*.

Sea Junk and Biscuits

Sailors would eat rats and even their own boots if a ship was long enough at sea and they got hungry enough.

Dampier's Dodgy Diary

According to Dampier the soil of New Holland was dry and sandy. None of its trees bore fruit or berries, there were few fish, but there were many manatees and turtles.

He also decided that the inhabitants were the most miserable people on the earth, and he described how they kept their eyes half-closed to keep the flies out. They had no houses, herbs, roots or grains to eat, tools, religion, nor any weapons except for 'wooden swords'.

The crew met Aboriginal people on the islands where they were stranded. When the sailors wanted to fill their barrels with fresh water, they gave some old ragged clothes to a group of Aboriginal men to wear, hoping they'd carry the barrels in return. They brought their 'new servants' to the spring, but the 'new servants' just grinned and refused to carry the water, so the sailors had to carry it themselves. Meanwhile, the islanders took off the clothes they had been given.

Most of what Dampier observed we know to be wrong. The people he saw did have tools, weapons and religion. They ate far better food than European sailors of the time—better even than most people in Britain. Dampier assumed what he saw was the whole of their lifestyle, but really he had seen only a glimpse.

Dampier's book became a best-seller in 1697 and made him famous as an expert of the 'South Seas'. But his descriptions of a barren land populated by poor and wretched inhabitants made Europeans less interested than ever in exploring New Holland.

Return of the Pirate

Because of the success of Dampier's book, the British Admiralty appointed him commander of an English Navy ship, the *Roebuck*, and ordered him to chart New Guinea and the east coast of New Holland, as well as to find *Terra Australis Incognita*—that unknown land of riches. New Holland may have been a barren place, but Dampier and the British Admiralty still believed that the Great South Land that Tasman had touched upon waited for them somewhere.

Even though much of Australia had been mapped by the Dutch, Holland and England were enemies, and so the Dutch maps weren't available to the English.

On arrival on the west coast of New Holland, Dampier sailed north from Shark Bay towards Roebuck Bay. His opinion of New Holland didn't improve. He then set off to hunt for the Southern Land with its gold and spices.

But the *Roebuck* was a rotten old ship. By the time Dampier had sailed around the north coast of New Guinea and arrived at the island called New Britain, the ship was leaking so badly that he had to turn back. The *Roebuck* eventually sank off an island in the Atlantic Ocean, but Dampier managed to save some of his papers and a few of the plants he'd collected.

On this trip Dampier succeeded in finding a strait between New Guinea and New Britain, north of New Guinea, but that was all. Furthermore, he concluded that the sections of New Holland he had spotted were only islands, and not part of the mainland at all. This conclusion led to one hundred years of confusion as people searched for the strait that was believed to separate the eastern and western parts of New Holland.

Dampier wrote more books, including one called *A Voyage to New Holland in 1699*. He also continued his career as both a pirate and a scientist.

DOUBLE VISION

As far as the Europeans were concerned, there were two southern lands: the barren New Holland, and *Terra Australis Incognita* with its gold and spices that Tasman was supposed to have discovered. But there were now lots of other things for most Europeans to worry about. The English concentrated on Indian trade, and on robbing Spanish ships carrying silver from Mexico to the Philippines. The Dutch had their spices in the Dutch East Indies, and the Spanish were busy in South America.

For Europeans, lands in the far south were places of romance and mystery. In 1726 the writer Jonathan Swift placed the imaginary land of Lilliput off the west coast of New Holland in his book *Gulliver's Travels*.

FRENCH NEW HOLLAND

Now the French were the only ones who kept looking for the mythical Great South Land. Louis Antoine de Bougainville saw the Great Barrier Reef in 1768—and kept well clear of it—before sailing north to New Guinea. In 1772 Louis Aleno de Saint-Allouarn sighted the south-west tip of Western Australia before he sailed north to Dirk Hartog Island and claimed the west coast of New Holland for France. Marc-Joseph Marion du Fresne landed on the south coast of Tasmania, and sailed around the island to the place where Tasman had landed.

But du Fresne didn't bother to follow the Australian coast north—he was far more interested in heading east to find the Great South Land. He sailed on to New Zealand—where he was eaten by Maori people he offended!

Nosing Around the Pacific

Much of Australia's coastline had now been seen and roughly mapped—and claimed for Holland and France—but none of the Dutch or French visitors had been interested enough to explore the land further. This was soon going to change. Both the English and the French were beginning to explore the Pacific region thoroughly—partly to extend their empires, partly for riches. But they also simply wanted to see what was there.

European tourists now spend thousands of dollars to holiday in the places that explorers rejected hundreds of years ago. Did the land really look so bad to these early explorers?

Those long-ago captains weren't looking for a place to take a holiday—or even for a place to start a farm. They wanted to trade for spices and gold, and they couldn't see evidence of either along the coasts of New Holland. They also needed safe harbours and deep rivers where their ships could shelter from storms—but along the New Holland coast it was hard even to find fresh water!

Australia just wasn't what they wanted at the time.

CHAPTER 10

THE RACE TO CONTROL THE PACIFIC

By the middle of the eighteenth century the Dutch trading empire was going downhill. Britain and France were enemies—and each was trying to claim more of the Pacific than the other. The English had been forced out of much of the Americas. But if the English could find—and hold—the mythical Great South Land, they'd be in a good position to control the rich trade of the Pacific, as well as trading furs from Canada and tea from China.

But France and Britain didn't only compete for trade—they competed for new knowledge, too.

Charting the Great Unknown

French and English voyagers had mapped many Pacific islands. But most of the Pacific—as well as the east coast of Australia and the Torres Strait—remained unknown until James Cook came along.

The old dream of a Great South Land was now combined with a growing interest in scientific knowledge, and it led to James Cook's voyage to the Pacific. And it was this voyage that led to him claiming the east coast of New Holland in the name of Britain and King George III.

James Cook, Grocer's Assistant

James Cook was born in a small village in North Yorkshire on 27 October 1728. He was the son of a labourer. Cook started out as a grocer's assistant. His career at sea began when he was eighteen and he became an apprentice on a collier, or coal ship. He worked his way up from apprentice to seaman, and from seaman to mate. In 1755 he was offered the command of a collier. But Cook turned it down.

Instead he enlisted in the Royal Navy as able-bodied seaman, the bottom rung of the navy career ladder. The English fleet was building up for war and there weren't enough trained seamen. James Cook was promoted quickly and, by 1757, he held the important position of master on a warship.

However, a master was a non-commissioned position, which meant he wasn't a real officer. To become an officer and to command his own ship, he needed a commission—and for that he needed money or an influential family. Cook had neither.

Cook's first experience of surveying and charting was on the *Pembroke* during General James Wolfe's campaigns against the French in Canada. Cook was part of the surveying team, and he made such a good impression that he was selected to survey the coast of Newfoundland when peace was declared in 1763.

Boys of twelve or even younger were regularly enlisted as captain's servants, cabinboys, ratings or seamen.

Cook spent the next four summers surveying Newfoundland, and each winter in London with his wife Elizabeth preparing his charts. These charts were so accurate and wide-ranging that they became standard maps.

Cook's Crew

It came as a surprise to some when James Cook was given command of an expedition to the Pacific in 1766. Cook was a brilliant surveyor, but his background was humble and he still had relatively little experience as a commander.

Unlike most voyages of exploration, this one was the combined project of the Royal Navy and the Royal Society. The Royal Society was a club of wealthy and, mostly, well-born scientists. James Cook was in charge of the ship, but the scientific part of the expedition was the responsibility of a wealthy young botanist, Joseph Banks.

Banks was accompanied by his scientific library, scientific equipment, and five assistants—the Swedish naturalist, Dr Daniel Solander; a secretary and draughtsman, Herman Spöring; two botanical artists, Alexander Buchan and Sidney Parkinson; and an astronomer, Charles Green—as well as his greyhounds. Banks also brought his personal musician to play for him while he ate.

Banks went to university, but like many gentlemen scholars he didn't finish his degree. However, he did spend three years at Oxford as a brilliant tutor.

Flower Power

In the days before cameras the best way to keep a record of a new plant was to paint its picture. For this reason, botanical artists were incredibly important on any voyage of discovery. Even today, botanical artists are able to draw parts of a plant that a camera won't pick up. Botanical artists can also include the bark, buds, flowers, seed capsules, and new and old leaves in the single drawing or painting—a combination that doesn't happen in real life for a camera to record.

Who's the Captain Around Here?

James Cook had many titles. According to his naval rank he was *Lieutenant* Cook. He was also referred to as *Captain* Cook (because he was captain of the ship) and *Commander* Cook (because he was in charge of the expedition). Cook was promoted to the naval rank of captain only after the voyage of HM Bark *Endeavour*.

Cook's Cooks

Navy cooks were usually sailors who were too crippled to do other work. The first cook assigned to the *Endeavour* for the 1770 voyage had only one leg—and didn't know how to cook. James Cook complained. So he was given a new cook—with only one hand! However, this one-handed cook, John Thompson, turned out to be very useful.

THE TRANSIT OF VENUS

The main reason the *Endeavour* was sailing to the Pacific Ocean was to measure how long it took the planet Venus to cross the face of the sun. This would help scientists work out how far Earth, Venus and the Sun were from each other. Ships' navigators needed to know exactly how far Earth was from the sun so they could work out where they were by looking at the stars. This is known as *celestial navigation.*

In 1769 the transit of Venus could be clearly seen from Tahiti in the Pacific Ocean. This would be the last opportunity to measure the transit until Venus crossed the sun again in 1874, 1882, 2004 and 2012.

MISSION INCREDIBLE

James Cook also had other orders—to search for the Great South Land. His instructions were to sail south from Tahiti to the latitude of 40°S, which was where this great continent was thought to be. If Cook didn't find the Great South Land, he was to head west and map as much as he could of the land that Tasman had discovered—New Zealand. He was to keep mapping until his provisions nearly ran out, then get back to a port where he could resupply for the return trip to England. New Holland wasn't mentioned in Cook's orders.

Myth: Captain Cook discovered Australia.

True story: Australia was discovered more than fifty thousand years ago—and quite a few more times after that.

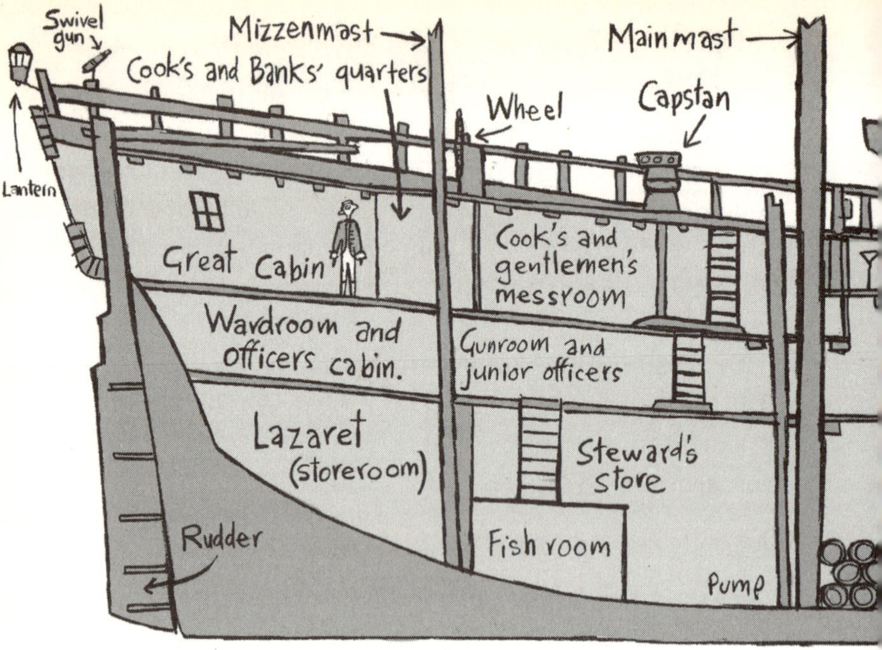

CHAPTER II

ON BOARD THE *ENDEAVOUR*

The *Endeavour* wasn't a navy ship. It was a Whitby collier—the same type of ship that James Cook had served his apprenticeship on. It had plenty of room for storage, and a *shallow draught*—which meant it could sail into shallow waters close to shore without hitting the bottom. Navy ships, on the other hand, were designed for the open seas and deep harbours.

The *Endeavour* sailed from Deptford, London, stopping in at Plymouth to pick up Joseph Banks and Dr Solander. They left England on Friday 26 August 1768 and sailed to Tahiti via the southern tip of South America. Then they watched the transit of Venus.

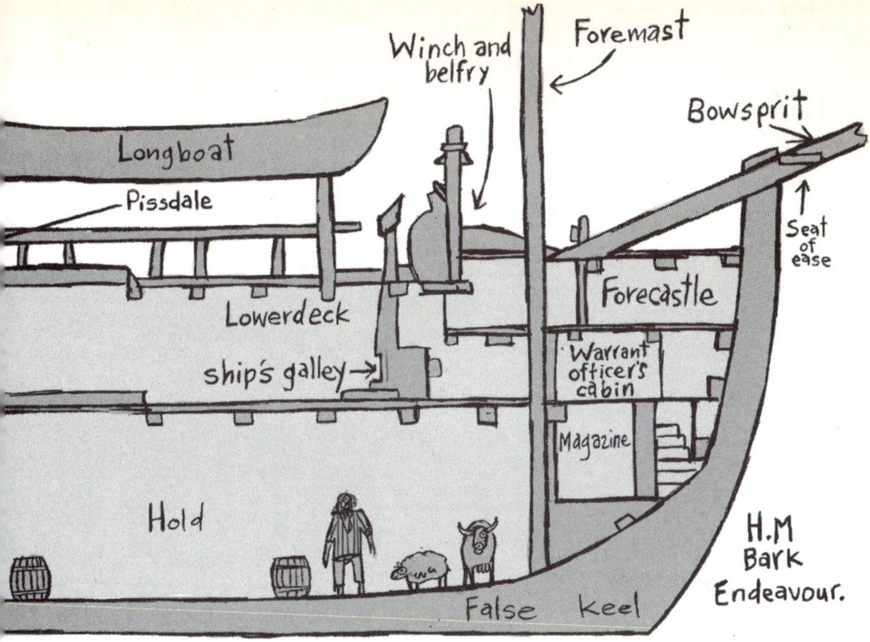

'NOPE, NUTHIN' HERE!'

Cook left Tahiti and sailed south. But although he sailed to the latitude of 40°S there was no land to be seen. And Cook could tell by the way the waves ran, and by the lack of land birds, that there was no land nearby.

Cook followed his orders and headed west to New Zealand. He mapped both islands, proving that they were separate and not connected to any continent. Then he hoisted the Union Jack on the island of Motuhora.

Cook took possession of the land in the name of King George III. The company then drank a bottle of wine and presented the empty bottle to an old man, one of the Maori who had accompanied them up the hill. Cook and his men told the Maori man that they were simply setting a mark on the island to show they'd been there—and not that they were claiming it for a foreign king, which was what they were really doing.

The Maori people confirmed for Cook what he already knew—that he had landed on an island.

One of Cook's crew, Tupaia, came from Tahiti. His language was close enough to Maori for him to talk to the people of New Zealand and interpret.

WESTWARD HO!

Cook then worked out what to do next.

He could sail back across the Pacific Ocean, find out if there really was a Great South Land out there in the ocean, and head home via Cape Horn. But the *Endeavour*'s sails had been badly damaged by gales off New Zealand—and the crew had only enough food for this journey if each man received no more than two-thirds of his normal rations.

Perhaps they could sail south, down around the bottom of Van Diemen's Land. But Cook decided this would be a waste of both time and stores, as he believed there was nothing new to find that way. He also doubted that the *Endeavour* would survive the fierce southern storms. There was only one alternative—to sail west to New Holland, and then north up the coast. He might as well map it as they went.

With luck they wouldn't have to go right up around the top of New Guinea. Joseph Banks had a copy of a chart that showed a strait between New Holland and New Guinea—the strait Luis Váez de Torres had found in 1606. If the chart was correct, it meant there was an easier way to get to Batavia for supplies and repairs on the way home.

But Cook would have to take his ship through uncharted waters to get there.

Aaarr! Them Scurvy Dogs!

Scurvy is a disease caused by not eating enough fruit and vegetables. It makes people's gums and legs swell, and their teeth fall out. They become too weak to move, and then they die. In the seventeenth and eighteenth centuries, scurvy killed more sailors than storms or shipwrecks did.

The Vikings, Chinese and Dutch took dried cranberries, potted ginger plants, spruce and pine shoots, sauerkraut and dried 'scurvy grass' with them on long voyages. They thought this would be enough fresh food for the sailors. Medical people of the time thought scurvy was caused by the stink on board ship, the lack of fresh meat, or bad salt used for storing the meat.

Even when naval surgeon Dr James Lind proved in 1747 that fresh fruit juice would cure scurvy, the British Admiralty ignored him. Fresh juice was too expensive, so the navy continued to hand out vinegar to prevent scurvy, even though it didn't help at all.

Cook was the first British naval officer to show that scurvy could be cured. He bought fresh vegetables at every port. When the crew ran out of fresh food, they ate boiled essence of lemons or oranges, sauerkraut and malt. None of Cook's crew died of scurvy, and when Cook got home he gave a talk to the Royal Society on how to keep sailors healthy. In return they presented him with the Society's annual prize, the Copley Medal, in 1776. But British sailors didn't regularly get lime or lemon juice as part of their diet until 1895.

A Different History?

Cook was going to map the east coast of Australia almost by accident. If there hadn't been wild New Zealand storms, or if Cook had visited New Zealand during another season, the history of Australia may have been very different.

CHAPTER 12

LANDFALL

The *Endeavour* left New Zealand from the peninsula Cook named Farewell Cape on 31 March 1770 and sailed across unknown seas to the uncharted east coast of New Holland.

Cook wanted to land on the south coast of Tasmania so he could start his maps where Tasman's map had finished. But southerly gales forced the *Endeavour* too far north for this—and Tasman's maps had been slightly wrong, too. Almost three weeks passed without actual sight of land, but the waves and the birds indicated there was land ahead.

On 18 April Cook ordered the topsails reefed so that the ship would travel more slowly and cautiously. They still couldn't see land, but if Tasman had been right it was there somewhere—and Cook was worried there might be reefs or rocks lurking under the waves.

When is a Reef Not a Reef?

Sailors *reef* a sail to reduce the area exposed to the wind. Large sailing ships have many reefing points that the sails are tied back to. Reefing is one of two ways of controlling the travelling speed of a ship. The other method is to alter the direction of the ship relative to wind direction so that the vessel *falls off the wind* and *spills* the wind from the sails.

Then, with first light on the morning of 20 April 1770, Lieutenant Zachary Hicks, Cook's second-in-command, saw land. It was five or six leagues distant (about thirty kilometres), while below the ship there was a fine sandy bottom, with no rocks or reefs. There was no sign of land to the south of them, although according to Tasman's map land should have been in sight. Cook was unable to tell if Van Diemen's Land was connected to the country he now saw, but because the coastline ran straight towards the west, Cook believed that he had found the southernmost point of some sort of landmass. Because his orders were to head back to England—and because he didn't have the resources to keep exploring south—he wasn't able to find out whether there was a link between this piece of coast and Van Diemen's Land.

What Cook saw was a green and hilly land covered by trees, with large stretches of sandy beach. There was also smoke—a sign that the country was probably inhabited.

Cook's first glimpse of New Holland was named Point Hicks after the lieutenant who spotted it. However, it turned out that Cook gave the wrong position for this sighting, which led to years of argument about where the first sighting of land on the east coast had actually been. In 1852 a surveyor named Smythe mapped the area and named the point Cape Everard. But in 1970 the Premier of Victoria, Henry Bolte, renamed it Point Hicks in honour of the Cook expedition. Point Hicks and its lighthouse are in what is now known as Croajingolong National Park.

Encounter at Stingray Harbour

The *Endeavour* sailed north, looking for a safe place to land. Cook named Cape Howe; then Mount Dromedary—because its hump looked like that of a camel. On 21 April they saw a bay that might give the ship shelter, but the wind was too strong to allow them to sail into it. Cook named it Batemans Bay after Captain Nathaniel Bateman, on whose ship Cook had once served.

On 22 April the crew spotted people on the shore for the first time, but only from a distance.

By now the crew badly needed both fresh food and water.

A week later, on the morning of 29 April, they found a sheltered bay. As they sailed into it they were able to get a closer look at the inhabitants of the land. The crew noted that the local people had very dark skin, and that they were naked. Some of the men had white powder on their faces and bodies, and were armed with long spears and strange curved wooden weapons. There were huts on both sides of the bay. There were also four canoes on the bay with men fishing from them using long spears.

The *Endeavour* dropped anchor near a village of bark huts. An old woman and some children came out from amongst the trees. The woman stared at the ship, but she didn't seem frightened or surprised. She lit a fire while the fishermen hauled their boats onto the shore. Then she began to cook dinner.

Go Away! Get Lost! Scarper!

That afternoon Cook ordered the boats manned. As the ship's boats neared the shore most of the villagers ran away—except for two men, one middle-aged and the other about nineteen. They waved their spears and woomeras and yelled, obviously telling the newcomers to go away.

There were only two of them against a party of forty sailors. Cook admired them for their courage. He asked Tupaia the Tahitian, who was still on board the *Endeavour*, to try to talk to them. But even though Tupaia had been able to understand Maori, he couldn't understand these people at all.

The sailors threw gifts of nails and beads to the two men to show they meant no harm and just wanted fresh water. The men seemed pleased, but when the newcomers came closer the men threatened them again.

Cook fired a musket between them. The younger man dropped his spears in shock, before picking them up again. The older man threw a stone at the boat. Cook ordered a musket with *small shot* to be fired. The shot hit the older man's leg, and he ran to one of the huts to fetch his shield. The two men then threw their spears at the landing party, but although the spears landed amongst Cook's men, no-one was hurt.

Small shot was made up of small pieces of metal that would scatter when fired from a musket. It didn't usually do a great deal of harm.

A third musket with small shot was fired. The men threw one more spear, then ran for the shelter of the trees. Cook wanted to chase and capture them, but Joseph Banks warned that their spears might be poisoned.

PONG-OH!

The people around Botany Bay were the Dharawal. Along with the people of the greater Sydney area, the Dharawal were also later known as the Eora (*Eora* means *here*, or *from this place*). Cook, however, left without learning the name of the people whose land he had visited.

There are no records to tell us what the local people thought of Cook's visit. But we can guess. The Dharawal probably thought the sailors were smelly, for a start. Few Europeans bothered to wash in those days, especially not with the limited water supply on board a ship. They'd also been eating rancid food and drinking stale water for almost a year—and that would have made their sweat even stinkier and their breath foul.

Most of the men would have had rotting teeth. The Dharawal people's teeth, on the other hand, would have been white and strong, and with their healthy lifestyle their bodies, too, would have been stronger and fitter than any of the visitors'.

Most of the crew were ragged. Even the officers and gentlemen in the party had no way of washing their clothes, much less ironing them. Official portraits done by the artists on board show the officers as clean and well-dressed, but the artists almost certainly prettied things up.

The ship itself must have been an astonishing sight—although the Dharawal may have heard stories about such ships that had been passed on from group to group along the trading routes. The noise of the weapons would have been terrifying—but though they may not have realised it at the time, the Dharawal weapons were in fact more accurate than the guns.

The newcomers would also have seemed ignorant about many basic things—such as knowing how to find fresh water, or which foods were good to eat. The Dharawal may also have wondered why the strangers covered their bodies with stinking cloth. And where their women were!

Isaac's Footprint

Now that the two local men had gone it was safe for the British to land. The first ashore was the young midshipman Isaac Smith, a cousin of Cook's wife, Elizabeth. Captain Cook had in fact been about to step ashore himself, but he stepped back and said, 'Isaac, you shall be first'.

Isaac Smith became the first white man to step onto the east coast of New Holland. He stepped ashore at what is now Kurnell in Botany Bay.

Cook and Banks's landing party went to peer into one of the huts. The children had hidden behind a shield, but the men moved so quietly that the children didn't seem to realise they'd been discovered.

Cook ordered his men to leave beads, ribbons and pieces of cloth in the hut to encourage the people to be friendly. He also ordered that all their spears be removed. Each spear had four sharp prongs of fishbone at the tip, which were covered in green stuff. Cook thought this green substance might be poison, but it turned out to be only seaweed: they were fishing spears, not weapons.

The landing party found no fresh water, except for some in a hole that had been dug in the sand. But when the party crossed to the north side of the bay they found a trickle of fresh water for drinking.

WANDERING IN THE WOODLAND

Over the next couple of days Cook, Banks, Dr Solander and seven others explored the country on the north side of the bay, towards present-day Maroubra. The country looked good—open grassed woodlands that could feed grazing animals; sandy but apparently fertile soil; and trees that looked like they'd provide good timber for houses and bridges. The explorers noted that some of the trees had been lopped with blunt axes, and that other trees had steps cut into the trunks to make them easier to climb.

They also saw a quadruped as small as a rabbit, which Banks's greyhounds almost caught—it was perhaps a small wombat, a pademelon or a bandicoot. The men were all struck by the exquisite beauty of the multitude of birds above them, as well as the waterbirds and the shellfish.

Tip-top Spot for a Colony, Chaps!

Cook's and Banks's descriptions of the country were so enthusiastic that they later inspired the British Government to establish a colony there. As well as praising the land itself, Cook made it clear that the local inhabitants wouldn't be a threat to settlement. There didn't seem to be many of them; they didn't live in 'societies'; and they were scattered about along the coast and in the woods. Perhaps, by describing the locals this way, Cook was trying to convince himself that there was no need to get their permission before claiming the land, as his orders required.

Cook and his men kept trying to make further contact with the local people, but after their experience with the muskets the locals kept well away. They didn't touch the gifts of mirrors, combs, beads, nails and cloth that the British left for them.

A Bay by Any Other Name…

It was on their final day that Cook named their landing place. On first arriving he'd named it Stingray Harbour because of the number of stingrays in the water. Now he renamed it after the plants that Banks and Solander had discovered—he called it Botany Bay.

British History Starts Here

Without realising it, Cook had laid the foundation for the next two centuries of European relations with the Indigenous people of Australia. For a start, Cook and the Dharawal had a complete lack of understanding of each other's culture. Also, the Dharawal had not been told that the British wanted to claim the land as their own—although Cook seems to have clearly understood that the locals didn't want the British there. Even so, the report that Cook wrote about his visit would soon inspire the British Government to send a fleet of convicts halfway around the world to found a colony there.

CHAPTER 13

HUGGING THE COAST

The *Endeavour* sailed out of Botany Bay on Sunday 6 May 1770, leaving behind the first British grave in Australia. It belonged to Forby Sutherland, who had died of tuberculosis and was buried at what is still called Point Sutherland.

By midday the *Endeavour* was outside the headlands of what would later become Sydney Harbour. Cook saw the harbour, noted that it seemed a safe anchorage, and called it Port Jackson. Then he sailed straight past.

Tuberculosis is a highly infectious disease that can attack any of the tissues of the body, forming small hard lumps. It is often a disease of the lungs, and is highly infectious when people live in crowded conditions—such as on board ship.

Over the next couple of weeks the ship continued slowly up the coast, with Banks and his men frantically trying to preserve all the specimens they'd gathered at Botany Bay. As they travelled further north, Cook named Mount Warning near what is now the New South Wales and

Queensland border. They named Moreton Bay, the Glasshouse Mountains and Sandy Cape; then on 23 May they anchored at Bustard Bay—named after the bustard they shot and ate for dinner—north of present-day Bundaberg.

By now they were trying to find their way through hazardous waters with sandbanks and rocks and dangerous tides. But the shallow-bottomed *Endeavour* survived.

Their next landing was at Thirsty Sound, where they found flocks of butterflies and great clouds of mosquitoes instead of the fresh water they so badly needed. But at least it was a chance to repair the ship. The sailors saw smoke and knew there must be people nearby, but they didn't meet any. Then they were off again, slowly and carefully working their way through the treacherous, unknown waters.

Treacherous Travelling

The ship was now between the mainland and the Great Barrier Reef, and Cook was intensely aware of the danger. The *Endeavour* was all alone, six months' sail from help. If the coral ripped a small hole in the hull they might be able to repair it—but if they were wrecked on the reef their only chance of survival would be in the ship's boats, and there wasn't room in them for the whole crew. The survivors would have to try to reach the Spice Islands in these small boats, sailing through totally unknown territory.

Danger in the Dark

Nights were the most dangerous time for sailing. Cook ordered the ship to proceed as slowly as possible, and for the lead to be dropped regularly to check the depth of the water.

Dropping the Lead

When ships passed through narrow or shallow waterways, it was vital to know the depth of the water. This was done by dropping a lead weight attached to a thin rope into the water and letting the lead sink to the bottom. The rope was marked at regular intervals along its length; by checking which mark was clear of the water, the sailor at the bow who was dropping the lead could see how deep the water was. He called out the depth to the helmsman, who used this information to navigate tricky waters. The measurements were taken in *fathoms*, which were equal to 1.8 metres.

During the day the *Endeavour's* boats went ahead, with sailors constantly peering into the water looking for submerged reefs, and dropping the lead to check the depth. At times the *Endeavour* had to wait while a smaller boat hunted out a channel between the banks of coral lurking beneath the surface.

North of Magnetic Island—so named because the compass swung wildly as they passed—Banks, Solander and Hicks went ashore to look for coconuts. But the palm trees they had spotted turned out to be cabbage palms, not coconut palms.

On 10 June Cook named Trinity Bay, where Cairns is today, and landed at Green Island, hoping to find fresh water, but not succeeding. They passed another cape, which Cook would later name Cape Tribulation—because that was where all his troubles began.

Shipwreck

The night of 11 June was fine and clear with a good breeze. Cook ordered the ship to sail further off-shore, as shoals were visible under the water and he was worried that they might run aground in the darkness. The water grew deeper and deeper, from fourteen to twenty-one fathoms, and everyone relaxed.

They were eating supper when suddenly twelve, ten and eight fathoms were reported, all within a few minutes. Cook ordered everyone to their stations to anchor ship. But suddenly the water grew deeper again. Cook decided that the danger was over. At ten o'clock the water was still twenty-one fathoms, and the crew went to bed feeling relaxed.

At eleven o'clock the water suddenly got shallower.

Then, without further warning, the ship struck a reef.

She was stuck fast, motionless but for the battering of waves about her. Everyone crowded onto the shuddering deck. Things looked grim. They were three-and-a-half hours' sail from shore.

The deck shook so much it was hard to stand. Wreckage floated about in the water, including the ship's false keel (the reinforcement attached to the true keel to protect it). It looked as though the bottom of the ship had been ripped apart.

Stuck Fast

No-one panicked. Cook ordered the sails furled, and the small boats to be put to sea so the damage could be investigated. They soon discovered that the *Endeavour* had run aground in a hollow in the reef, with shallow water all around her. Not only that, but there was a great gaping hole in the hull, and it was getting bigger all the time.

It was high tide, and they knew that as the tide dropped the ship would sink further down into the hollow and become more firmly wedged. Cook ordered the crew to throw everything they could overboard to lighten the ship. This included the six great guns on deck; iron and stone ballast; casks; hoop staves; oil jars and decayed food supplies.

Every man knew that the situation was desperate—so desperate, Cook wrote years later, that the crew even stopped swearing.

Twixt Hell and High Water

It was a terrible night. They all felt the ship grinding on the coral below them. She couldn't hold together for long. But the ship didn't break up in the darkness. Daylight came. They could see land in the distance, about forty kilometres away.

The ship's boats would not carry the whole crew. If there had been an island nearby the boats could have made several journeys to ferry the crew to safety. But there were no islands. Everyone knew that most of the crew would probably drown. Those who survived faced an unknown shore.

Then the wind dropped, leaving a dead calm. If the wind had stayed strong the waves would have battered the ship to pieces, but at least now they stood a chance. They threw off another fifty tonnes of material and waited for the tide to rise. The water rose about them. Would the *Endeavour* lift with the tide, or was she stuck?

The ship stayed firm. The two pumps were only just enough to keep her from flooding. By two o'clock the *Endeavour* was leaning badly to one side.

Desperate Measures

There was only one option—to use block-and-tackle to haul the ship off the reef at the high tide. Meanwhile, the leak increased. Two more pumps were manned, but only one of them worked. The ship slowly righted herself as the tide came in—but the leak increased even more. Surely the ship would sink, even if it floated free.

The crew waited for death. Cook knew that as soon as the ship began to sink his authority would vanish—the men would be fighting, and killing, for a chance at the boats and life.

The ship lifted higher and higher still. Suddenly, at twenty minutes past ten, she floated free. But water was flooding through the hole. And the men were exhausted. They had been pumping for twenty-four hours without a break. One by one they fell unconscious.

Finally the man measuring the water in the hull yelled that the water was rising! Despite their efforts they were doomed . . .

But they weren't. The man had made a mistake: he'd measured the height of the water in the hold from the outside, not on the inside of the hull. That mistake may have saved the crew's lives. As soon as they knew that the water was lower—and not higher—they felt a sudden surge of hope and redoubled their efforts.

But they couldn't keep going for much longer. And there seemed to be no way to get the ship to shore so it could be mended.

Poo To the Rescue

Then Mr Monkhouse, a midshipman, proposed that they try something he had seen done on board a merchant ship. He suggested they sew oakum (fibres picked from old rope) and wool onto one of the sails, then spread it with sheep's dung and other filth—probably their own faeces. The wool and oakum would swell when wet, and the dung would seal and waterproof it. The sail would then be dragged across the hole in the hull. This was called *fothering* the ship.

On 13 June Cook put Monkhouse in charge of the operation. The sailors sewed on the wool and oakum, smeared it with dung, then guided the sail under the ship with chains until it was positioned across the hole. The pressure of water flowing into the hull washed the sail into the hole and blocked it.

But would it save the *Endeavour*?

The man who saved the *Endeavour* and changed the course of history later died of dysentery in Batavia on the way home to England. But without Monkhouse, the *Endeavour* would have been lost—and Australia would probably never have been settled by the British.

Limping Ashore

Cook sent the small boats out to find a safe landing place. When a river mouth was discovered, Cook went to check it himself to make doubly sure it was safe. The river is now called the Endeavour River, and Cooktown stands there today.

On 18 June, nearly a week after striking the reef, they finally got the *Endeavour* to the shore. Wind and high seas slowed them down, and the men had to take it in turns to pump all the way. The *Endeavour* ran aground again as she entered the river mouth, but not seriously. Finally they moored her safely next to a steep beach, where they could check the damage to her hull at low tide.

On Friday 22 June they hauled the *Endeavour*'s bow close to the shore so it would be above water at low tide. When the tide went out they laid the ship over and inspected her hull. Cook discovered they had been saved by a miracle. The damage was even worse than they had thought. Parts of the keel and false keel were gone, as well as the sheathing to the bow. There was also more than one hole—and they discovered that the biggest hole was plugged by a piece of coral as large as Cook's fist. If the coral had fallen out the ship may have sunk.

The ship's carpenters and blacksmiths started work at once.

Bizarre Beasts

On 23 June Cook sent out a hunting party to shoot pigeons so that the sick could have some fresh food. While these men were in the bush they saw what they described as a swift hopping animal, the size of a greyhound and the colour of a mouse. They later learnt that the locals called this hopping animal a *kangaroo*.

One of the men from the shooting party declared he had seen the devil. It was big and black, with horns and wings. But the 'devil' turned out to be just a giant bat—probably a flying fox.

Befriending the Locals

On 10 July the shipwrecked crew finally met some local people—whom we now know belonged to the Guugu Yimithirr language group. Four men were spearing fish from a canoe near a sandy point on the river. Cook waited until they brought their canoe close to where the ship rested, then instructed the sailors to throw them gifts of cloth, nails, beads, paper and a fish. The men in the canoe made hand signals saying they would fetch their friends, then paddled back to the shore.

They soon returned with others and sat for a while with members of the crew. The local men didn't leave until they were invited in sign language to join the crew for dinner on the ship, at which point they left.

Four men came back the next day, bringing a present of a large fish. One of them introduced himself as Yaparico. He had a thick bone stuck through his nose. The others had holes through their noses too, but without bones, and their ears were pierced. They wore bracelets of plaited hair, and nothing else.

From then on the crew often saw the local inhabitants, and Cook, Banks and Monkhouse made notes about everything. As well as bones and bracelets, many of the locals wore bark tied across their foreheads; two of them wore necklaces of shells that they refused to give away. The British noted how the canoes had outriggers like the ones they had seen in Tahiti, and that these canoes were worked with poles in shallow water and with metre-long paddles in deep water.

Cook was startled by how powerful the spears and woomeras were. One man threw a spear which pierced a tree about fifteen metres away. Cook wrote that the spear must have been carefully crafted and balanced in order to be accurate over such a great distance.

Turtle Trouble

The two groups of people—the locals and the newcomers—remained on friendly terms for about a week. Then things changed.

On 19 July a party of locals came aboard to ask if they could have some of the turtles the crew had caught. Joseph Banks refused to give them any. Two of the local men grabbed a couple of turtles anyway. The crewmen snatched the turtles back. Cook offered the men some bread instead but they angrily rejected it.

The locals paddled back to shore, took a piece of burning wood from the fire and used it to light the tall grass in the *Endeavour* camp. Luckily the ship's gunpowder had been taken back on board—if it had exploded, the crew of the *Endeavour* would have lost everything. In the fire that followed, a piglet was scorched to death and the blacksmiths' forge was damaged. Meanwhile the locals set fire to more grass where the *Endeavour*'s fishing nets and linen were drying. Cook ordered his men to fire with small shot. Then Cook himself shot one of the ringleaders. He didn't think he had badly wounded the man, but they never knew for sure.

Later that day a small group of locals approached the camp, led by an old man carrying a spear without a point. Cook believed this was a sign of peace. The man's companions left their spears against a tree, and the crew of the *Endeavour* returned those spears that they had taken. There was no more fighting. But from then on the local people refused to board the *Endeavour*.

The first blood had been spilt. In years to come there would be much more.

Culture Clash

The two groups totally misunderstood each other. The local people traditionally shared their food, and they must have thought the British were selfish and unfriendly when they wouldn't share the turtles. By refusing to share, the British had behaved like enemies—and fire was a traditional weapon against enemies. The crew didn't need the turtles: they had all the turtles they could eat. They just didn't like the way the local people took 'their' property.

It seems like a lot of fuss about nothing. But over the next two centuries, small misunderstandings like this would lead to great tragedy.

CHAPTER 14

FAREWELL, NEW HOLLAND

It took seven weeks to repair the ship. Then bad weather kept the expedition at the Endeavour River for a further two weeks. Cook wasn't looking forward to the journey to the Spice Islands. He had climbed the tallest hill in the area and seen that the passage to the north was full of rocks, reefs, shoals and islands. He was worried that they'd never find their way through without disaster.

The crew stocked the ship with fish, shellfish, stingrays, turtles, sharks and green vegetables. After a couple of false starts they finally set sail on 6 August. As they left the coast, Cook and several other officers kept a lookout, climbing the masthead to see if they could spot a way through the reef.

But things looked bad. Waves crashed against the reefs for as far as they could see. At low tide it was easy to see the reefs, as the waves breaking over them showed where danger lay,

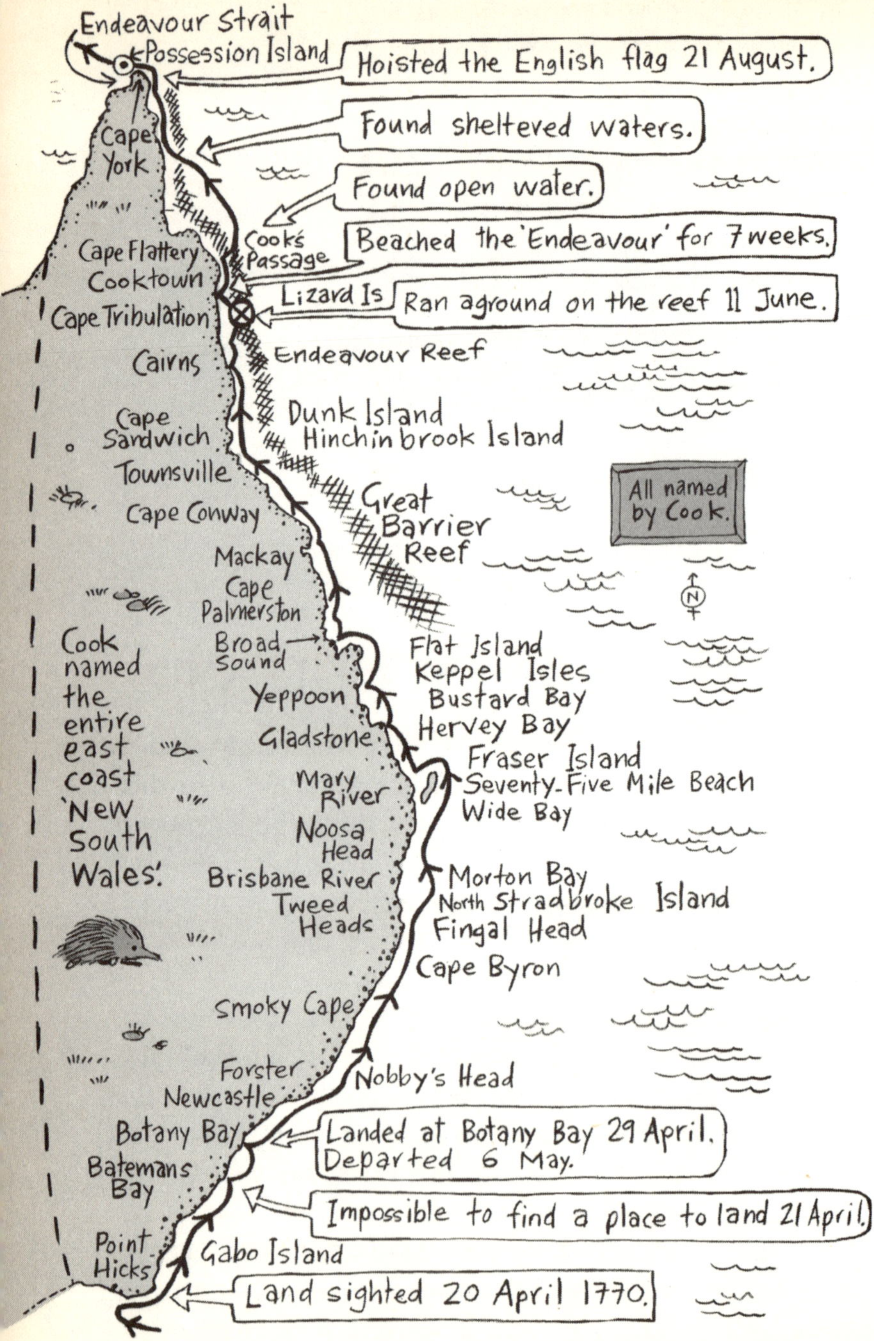

Endeavour Strait
Possession Island
Hoisted the English flag 21 August.
Found sheltered waters.
Found open water.
Cape York
Cook's Passage
Beached the 'Endeavour' for 7 weeks.
Cape Flattery
Cooktown
Lizard Is
Ran aground on the reef 11 June.
Cape Tribulation
Endeavour Reef
Cairns
Dunk Island
Hinchinbrook Island
Cape Sandwich
Townsville
All named by Cook.
Cape Conway
Great Barrier Reef
Mackay
Cape Palmerston
N
Broad Sound
Flat Island
Keppel Isles
Bustard Bay
Hervey Bay
Cook named the entire east coast 'New South Wales'.
Yeppoon
Gladstone
Fraser Island
Seventy-Five Mile Beach
Wide Bay
Mary River
Noosa Head
Brisbane River
Morton Bay
North Stradbroke Island
Tweed Heads
Fingal Head
Cape Byron
Smoky Cape
Forster
Newcastle
Nobby's Head
Botany Bay
Landed at Botany Bay 29 April. Departed 6 May.
Batemans Bay
Impossible to find a place to land 21 April.
Point Hicks
Gabo Island
Land sighted 20 April 1770.

but at high tide the sea was smooth and there was no way of telling where the reefs were lurking. The master suggested they go back towards the south—the way they'd come before the shipwreck. Cook said no: if they went back they'd have to battle the strong wind coming from the south. But if they went onwards to the north they might be trapped by reefs and have to turn back anyway. Cook could only hope there would be a way ahead through the reef.

Trapped by the Reef

One of the ship's small boats, a *pinnace*, went ahead sounding for a safe passage through the shoals, and the *Endeavour* followed. Over the next few days they sailed slowly north. Cook landed at Point Lookout to climb a hill and search for a channel through the reef, and the next day they sailed out to Lizard Island on the edge of the reef. Here Cook and Banks again climbed a hill. From this lookout they could see rocks and crashing surf, but there also appeared to be channels between the rocks to the north-east that led out to what seemed like open sea.

Cook now had to decide whether they should head out to sea or keep sailing north up the inside of the reef. If they stayed within the reef, would they end up trapped by its shoals of sand and coral? They had less than three months' worth of food supplies—if they couldn't get to Batavia within three months they'd starve.

So Cook decided to head through the channel and out to sea—even though this meant they wouldn't be able to map the rest of the coast. They might not even be able to prove whether or not there was a strait between New Holland and New Guinea.

Channel Surfing

Once they were safely through the channel, the ocean swell that ran from the south-east showed Cook there were no more rocks or shoals—they'd made it safely through the reef. The crew watched the giant surf beating on the reef to their left. There was 150 fathoms of water below the ship, and for the first time in three months they didn't have to worry about lurking rocks.

For a couple of days they sailed north, out of sight of land, then headed west towards land again, because Cook was afraid they'd overshoot the strait between New Holland and New Guinea. But now there was another danger. The waves of the open sea started to drive the *Endeavour* back towards the reef—the wind had dropped, leaving the ship dangerously close to rocks and mountainous surf, with no way of steering clear; and the water was too deep to drop anchor. But the next day, after struggling to keep the ship clear of the terrible surf, they at last they found another channel—Providential Channel—which got them back to the calm water between the reef and the shore.

Getting to the Point

Once again they wound their way north between the rocks and islands of the reef, charting the coastline and sending the ship's boats (a *yawl* and the pinnace) ahead to hunt for the safest route for the big ship to follow. Finally, on Tuesday 21 August, the *Endeavour* sailed around the northernmost point of the continent. Cook named it Cape York. From this point on, the coastline dipped towards the south-west, and Cook knew he had found the passage to the Indian Ocean—the Torres Strait. The ship would make it home—and Cook had confirmed that New Holland was separate from New Guinea.

Staking a Claim

Cook believed he'd charted the entire east coast of New Holland. He had named the most prominent capes and mountains visible from the sea, made meticulous notes, and at Botany Bay he had left details of the ship and date of landing. It was now time to take formal possession of the country in the name of King George III. The *Endeavour* anchored by an island west of Cape York. Cook, Banks, Solander and others of the crew went ashore.

The island was inhabited. As the visitors approached, they saw ten men, nine of whom were armed with spears and the tenth with a bow and arrows. Cook expected the men to prevent them landing, but the islanders simply walked calmly away.

The party from the *Endeavour* landed, climbed the tallest hill and gazed around. To the north-west they saw islands, to the east was the mainland, and to the west and south-west there was nothing but open sea. By now Cook had no doubts about the Torres Strait.

Cook once more hoisted the British flag and, in the name of King George III, took possession of the whole eastern coast of New Holland from Point Hicks in the south to the Torres Strait in the north, including all the bays, harbours, rivers, and islands. He renamed it New South Wales. The men fired three volleys, which were answered with three volleys fired from the ship. Cook named the island Possession Island.

Mapping it Makes it Mine

A ceremony on an island hilltop may not seem much of a way to claim half a continent. But those were the days when up-to-date maps were vitally important, and Cook had mapped an enormous area of the Pacific. To draft maps of the places where he'd travelled proved that he'd really been there—and he could therefore also prove that he had claimed these places for his country. Cook's maps of New South Wales would firmly establish British right to this land in the eyes of all seafaring Europeans. Of course, the ceremony Cook performed on Possession Island wouldn't have any impact on the rest of the world—including the people who actually lived in New South Wales. But that wasn't important. However, keeping New South Wales from the Dutch and the French was very important indeed.

What's in a Name?

Of all the names that Captain Cook gave to the places, plants and animals of New South Wales, only one—*kangaroo*—was a local word. All the other names were European. Places were usually named after European people, and plants and animals were named according to European, Caribbean, Indian or African plants and animals that they happened to look like.

'Owners? What Owners?'

James Cook proclaimed that the east coast of New Holland belonged to the British. He did this even though he knew there were already people living there—and despite the fact that he knew those people didn't want the British around.

Cook's orders had been to seek the approval of the locals before making any claims. In spite of this, Cook went ahead as though there was no-one there. That is, he declared New South Wales to be *terra nullius*—and belonging to no-one . . . until he claimed it.

Cook saw the local people as 'primitive', which, in his eyes, meant they had no culture, no organised government, no civilisation. According to Cook they moved about the country like 'wild beasts', and neither owned nor farmed any of it.

Cook believed that most of the country was empty. The largest group of locals he had seen so far consisted of only ten people. He also knew that the west coast of New Holland was dry, so he assumed that only the east coast was lush, and that the rest of the land would be too barren for people to be living in.

Cook was mostly wrong. But even if he had understood more about the people and places he had visited, he would probably have claimed it for Britain all the same. According to the European custom of the time, Cook could claim Australia simply because it didn't have a king or queen of its own.

CHAPTER 15

HEADING HOME

Cook's final Australian landing-place was on tiny Booby Island in the Torres Strait, where the ocean swell coming from the west convinced him that they were indeed headed towards the Indian Ocean.

After leaving New Holland, the *Endeavour* sailed along part of the south coast of New Guinea before heading to the Spice Islands. The ship was repaired and refitted, and the stores were replenished for the long voyage to England. Here, sadly—after two years with almost no loss of life—tropical diseases took the lives of many of the crew. Only fifty-six of the original crew of ninety-four reached home, two years and eleven months after their journey began.

BEST-SELLING COOK-BOOK

Cook's and Banks's diaries were combined and published as a single book. Their description of New South Wales changed the European idea of what New Holland was like. New South Wales wasn't a barren desert like the west coast. The land seemed fertile, the timber good, grass and game abundant. Best of all, there were good harbours where ships could anchor safely. It even looked as though a settlement could survive there.

Although New South Wales didn't have gold mines, spices or other exciting merchandise, it still seemed fascinating to British readers. The British were also entranced by the new plants that Banks had brought back, as well as the portraits of the New South Wales locals, and the animal and insect specimens.

Most interesting of all, the Aboriginal inhabitants of New South Wales seemed to fit in with a trendy idea of the time—the idea of the *noble savage*. The Aboriginal people appeared to live a simple, ideal life without having to worry about money or working long hours. It seemed that they weren't even interested in possessions, as they couldn't have cared less about the gifts Cook offered them.

For many years people had believed what Dampier said about the people of New Holland—that they were the most wretched beings on earth—which wasn't true. Now these same Indigenous people were assumed to have a beautifully simple life—which wasn't entirely true either.

Who Owned Australia?

The Portuguese?

In 1493 the Pope gave Portugal the half of the world that included eastern Australia.

The Dutch?

By 1770 the Dutch had claimed the western, northern and southern coastlines of the continent.

The British?

Cook claimed the east coast in 1770.

The French?

In 1772 the French claimed the west coast.

The Indigenous People?

Many nations of Indigenous people had already been living there for tens of thousands of years.

And That's Not All . . .

James Cook explored and mapped more of the earth's surface than any other person in history. After his voyage to New Holland he made two more great exploratory voyages. He was the first to enter the Antarctic Circle, and he visited Hawaii, Norfolk Island, New Caledonia and many other places in the Pacific. He spent a year sailing back and forth across the South Pacific, eventually working out that there was no great southern continent there. The mythical land of gold didn't exist.

Is It, or Isn't It?

James Cook visited Van Diemen's Land on his final voyage in 1777, on his way from the Indian Ocean to the Pacific Ocean (on his quest to find the North-West Passage in Alaska!). He called in partly to rest the crew after the ship was caught in fogs and gales in the Southern Ocean; partly to restock with fresh water and food for the animals; and partly to see whether Van Diemen's Land was joined to New Holland.

On 26 January 1777 he anchored his ship, the *Resolution*, in Adventure Bay. The crew collected fresh grass for the animals, wood for the stoves and fresh water to drink, as well as meeting some of the local people. But the journey was behind schedule, so as soon as the wind picked up, Cook sailed for New Zealand.

The mystery of whether Van Diemen's Land was part of New Holland remained unsolved.

THREE LITTLE PIGS

Cook wanted to leave a young bull, a cow and some sheep and goats in Van Diemen's Land so they would breed, multiply and become a supply of fresh meat for other visiting sailors. But he thought that the local inhabitants might eat them, so he decided against it. However, he did leave three pigs.

The pigs of Van Diemen's Land didn't survive. But the pigs that Cook had left at Endeavour River, northern Queensland, became feral and flourished.

THE DEATH OF CAPTAIN COOK

On his third voyage of exploration, Cook's mission was to find a north-west passage from the Pacific Ocean to the Atlantic Ocean. He spent a summer trying vainly to find this passage, then headed south to Hawaii for the winter, where he arrived in January 1779.

For a couple of weeks his crew and the Hawaiian people got along well, but after a series of small thefts, things became hostile. Cook ordered his men to fire *ball shot* at the Hawaiians if they threw stones or behaved insolently. This was unlike Cook. He'd always made a point of ordering small shot fired as a warning, and not ball shot, which could kill.

When one of the ship's boats was stolen Cook went ashore to demand that the local king come on board to sort the matter out. The king agreed, but an argument broke out when a growing crowd pleaded with the king not to go.

No-one is sure what happened next. But in the anger and confusion shots were fired. Cook was clubbed from behind as he waved the ship's boats to come in, then he was stabbed in the neck by one of the ship's iron daggers, given in trade to the islanders. More blows followed, and Cook's body vanished into the blood-stained water. The officers of his ship demanded their captain's body back, but they were given only a slice of his thigh. The remainder of his body was sent to various important chiefs, or else burnt.

Parts of Cook's body were eventually sent back, wrapped in a feathered cape. The hands were recognisable by a scar, and had been slashed open and packed with salt to preserve them.

THE MYSTERY OF HM BARK *ENDEAVOUR*

The *Endeavour* was originally a collier. She was two years old when she was bought by the Admiralty for Cook's first expedition. She was thirty-two metres long, almost nine metres wide at her widest point, and had a hold three metres deep. She didn't have a smart figurehead—she was a working ship, and looked it.

Her first name was the *Earl of Pembroke*, but she was renamed the *Endeavour* after being fitted out by the Navy in preparation for her long voyage. After the *Endeavour*'s voyage with Cook she was used as a storeship and made three trips to the Falkland Islands in the south Atlantic before being sold in 1775. Then she went back to hauling coal in the North Sea.

What happened to the *Endeavour* after that remained a mystery for years. Did she end up as a prison hulk for female convicts on the Thames? Or was that another ship with the same name? Was she bought as a whaler, renamed the *Liberté* and run aground at the US port of Newport? Or had that been Cook's later ship, the *Resolution*?

In 1776 it was reported that an *Endeavour* of 355 tonnes (Cook's *Endeavour* was 374 tonnes), originally built at Whitby in 1764, had been repaired and renamed the *Lord Sandwich*. In 1779, the *Lord Sandwich* disappeared from the records.

Conclusion

Land of Lost History

Australia had at least fifty thousand years of human history before the Europeans arrived. That history included an empty land becoming a land of many nations; the rising of seawater that drowned the coasts; land bridges submerging to isolate Tasmania from the mainland, and the mainland from the rest of the world; and animal species disappearing and new ones arriving. But the stories of this history were never written down, and while many were passed on orally, many others were lost once the Europeans arrived and the Aboriginal people became homeless in their own land.

Human history on the continent changed gradually over the millennia, but when the Europeans arrived a lot happened very fast. The brief visits of explorers in the sixteenth, seventeenth and eighteenth centuries were soon to turn into a very long visit indeed—beginning in 1788. Then, in just over a hundred years, the ancient land of many nations would become one nation—Australia.

INDEX